T5-DGI-444

Managing Expert Systems

Managing Expert Systems

Nigel Bryant
Cranfield School of Management

JOHN WILEY & SONS
Chichester • New York • Brisbane • Toronto • Singapore

British Library Cataloguing in Publication Data:
Bryant, Nigel
Managing expert systems.
1. Management—Data processing
2. Expert systems (Computer science)
I. Title
006.3'3'024658 HD30.2

ISBN 0 471 91341 3

Library of Congress Cataloging in Publication Data:
Bryant, Nigel (Nigel W.)
Managing expert systems/Nigel Bryant.
p. cm.
Bibliography: p.
Includes index.
ISBN 0 471 91341 3 (pbk.) :
1. Expert systems (Computer science) I. Title.
QA76.76.E95B78 1988
006.3'3'–dc19

Printed and bound in Great Britain by
Biddles Ltd, Guildford and King's Lynn

Contents

Preface

A great deal of personal computing is about promises, most as yet unrealised. The current promise is expert systems. But this is an offer being pushed by the suppliers and not necessarily asked for by the users. There are several possible reasons why expert systems are not more widespread. Firstly, it may be because they are inherently useless. Secondly, they are not yet well known and publicised. I prefer to believe the latter, expert systems are useful but have yet to achieve a place in a manager's software library. Hence this book, which was written particularly for managers and students of management, although it may give data processing managers a new view of the world. It attempts to give a readable and realistic view of what expert systems are and how they can be used.

Each chapter is independent, although in a carefully chosen order, and can be read in isolation. Those readers looking for a cursory glance at expert systems can read Chapters one, two, six, seven, and ten. Those trying to choose a shell to purchase can concentrate on Chapters seven, eight, nine, ten and eleven. Anybody wishing to go through the complete process of purchasing, developing, implementing and using a system should find all chapters of interest.

Any author is indebted to a wide group of people and I would like to express my gratitude to all those who contributed to this book. I am grateful to Epson (UK) for the loan of the hardware necessary to run the systems described in this book. I also extend gratitude to all the software suppliers who gave me the opportunity to test their products, in particular Database Experts Limited and Intelligent Terminals Limited for the examples given in Chapters six and ten. Helen Corless deserves a special mention for reading and giving valuable advice on the various drafts of this book. All remaining errors and omissions are, of course, my responsibility. Thank you to Elizabeth, my wife, for her tolerance and patience and, finally, a few words to Louise, Jonathan and Sam: Daddy is no longer 'working on his book'.

NIGEL BRYANT
Cranfield School of Management
Bedford
June 1987

1
An Introduction to Expert Systems

INTRODUCTION

During the working day a manager will ask a variety of questions such as: Why are sales falling in South America? What is happening to production in China? Should we appoint x? What are the implications of a particular course of action? These questions reflect the way we think and question the world. Unfortunately, computers do not think in the same way. Using a traditional computer application requires the user to adopt the style of the computer rather than vice versa. Thus existing software packages that you are likely to be using in your organisation, such as spreadsheets, databases and text processors, use information structured in a particular way to suit the package. Artificial intelligence (AI) is an area of computing that attempts to create machines that will perform in the same way as humans.

Whilst still in its infancy, AI is starting to live up to some of its early promises. This is most evident in the recent addition to the range of packages available for managers to use on their personal computers: expert systems.

Such systems are seen as the growth area of the late 1980s. We have had the era of the spreadsheet, the word processor and, currently, the database; next, it is argued, we will have the era of the expert system. Estimates of the increase in the number of expert systems vary according to the pundit; but there is general agreement that a boom is due. It has been suggested that by 1990 the European market for expert systems will be two and a half billion pounds with the UK accounting for nearly one hundred and eighty millions of this market. Furthermore, the number of applications will double each year, based on 1986 figures, which means that by 1990 there will be sixteen times the current number of applications. In Europe, this increase is due largely to the advent of small systems running on personal computers. In the US the growth is equally large but more effort and emphasis is directed at larger scale systems. What large and small expert systems are and what they can do for managers is the subject of this book. Meanwhile, let us start with a brief review of the history leading to expert systems as we know them today.

A BRIEF HISTORY OF ARTIFICIAL INTELLIGENCE

There are both quantitative and qualitative differences between computers and human beings. Computers can perform millions of mathematical calculations per second, far in excess of their human users. Processing power, that is the ability to perform such calculations, apparently has no limit. However, the quantity of calculations is not reflected in the quality of what a computer can do. There is still an enormous gap between what a computer can do and what a human can do.

This may seem surprising given the perceived power of computers. Imagine for a moment the everyday tasks performed by a human that could not be done by a computer: the shelling of a boiled egg, changing a nappy, identifying a sock in a drawer of odd socks, playing tennis. All of these tasks require a combination of three things: taking in information from the outside world, making intelligent choices about what to do based on the enormous and complex knowledge we have stored somewhere, and, finally, manipulating the outside world using coordinated hand/eye movements. That is not to say that these tasks will not be performed by a computer one day.

Attempts have been made to replicate the way humans solve problems. In the 1950s the general problem solving (GPS) model was developed. The aim was to create a model which reasoned intelligently and solved all the problems asked of it. Further such a GPS would have inbuilt intuition and the ability to learn from its successes and mistakes. Unfortunately such an approach was doomed to failure. This attempt at what we would now call artificial intelligence was simply trying to do too much at once.

The breakthrough came when researchers started to consider each problem as a separate issue and tackle each individually. Thus the 1960s and 1970s saw the development of knowledge based systems that were applied in one area. Such applications included Dendral, a system for identifying molecular structure; Mycin, a system to diagnose and give treatment plans for infectious blood diseases; and R1, a package developed by Digital Equipment to enable people to configure their computer systems. These large packages will be discussed in more detail later. The field of artificial intelligence is now divided into a collection of smaller, more manageable areas of research and application. Following the success of large knowledge-based systems, smaller scale expert systems have been developed which form the basis for this book.

However, there are those who would argue that we are moving away from artificial intelligence and developing systems that do not comply with the notion at all. We need to define intelligence. Is it an ability to solve problems, to be creative, to communicate with others or, more esoterically, our notion that we have consciousness, that makes us humans intelligent and different to the rest of the animal kingdom? Extending the problem, how can we say that a machine is acting intelligently? We can use 'The Turing Test', postulated by Alan Turing, an English mathematician and pioneer in the field of computing and artificial intelligence, before his untimely death in 1954, at the age of 41. He argued that a machine is acting intelligently if it can convince a human user conversing with it via a computer terminal that it is not a computer. Playing chess against a remote opponent it may be difficult for the player to decide if he or she is in conflict with a human or a computer program. Here the important test is not can the computer play a good game and win (I have just been beaten by a chess playing computer!). Rather, can the computer convince me it is human, for example, can it lose without making obviously silly moves; the sort of game we play with our children and grandchildren to boost their confidence? I suspect the ability to win convincingly is easier to replicate than the ability to lose with conviction.

At the heart of current artificial intelligence systems is a body of knowledge stored in the computer which is accessible to both the computer and the users. Unfortunately, there is no consistent thought about how that knowledge should be represented. We do not have a unifying theory of knowledge based on a great person's ideas, like relativity has Einstein, gravity has Newton and gases have Boyle. We can accept the notion that a machine should 'fool all the people all the time' but how does it store the knowledge to do it? There are two schools of thought.

Firstly there are neats who believe that there are underlying general priniciples of artificial intelligence which can be built into a system

Figure 1: *Neats vs Scruffies*

using formal, predicate logic that is structured and testable. Such advocates support PROLOG, an assertional language used for storing relationships between objects, for example, Bob is the father of Harry, and for drawing inferences from those relationships. PROLOG is described more fully in Chapter six. Opposing the neats are the scruffies who perceive human intelligence as a much looser system of heuristics or ad-hoc rules with little or no underlying structure. Their approach is exemplified in LISP, a symbol manipulating language, written particularly to handle lists. LISP is dominant in the USA compared with PROLOG which is a European phenomenon.

Given our imperfect knowledge of humans, their knowledge storage systems (memory) and intelligence, we are unlikely to resolve the neats versus scruffies debate. Meanwhile people working in the area of artificial intelligence are building expert systems based largely on sets of rules or heuristics and are following a scruffy approach, although, to complicate the issue, some are written in PROLOG. As our understanding of ourselves increases and we ascertain the underlying rules and structure of our brain/mind/intelligence we may be able to be 'neater' in our modelling of humans using computers. The current answer is a combination of structure and looseness. The fifth generation of computers, that is, the next advance in computing currently being built in Japan, probably will use a combination of neat and scruffy principles.

Whilst emphasis has been placed on reasoning and intelligence, other areas of artificial intelligence have been pursued. Considerable attention has been given to the development of robotic systems. Again the original notion was to create a complete mechanical/electrical substitute for a human being, that is a robot. This notion has been temporarily abandoned for smaller scale robots that perform particular tasks, such as welding a particular part of a car, making tea or defusing bombs. Eventually it is possible that all the various manual skills will be combined in one humanoid form. Until then, robots continue to give tireless, accurate, repetitive service without tea breaks, holidays or strikes.

THE CHANGING NATURE OF TECHNOLOGY

Mention was made earlier of the fifth generation of computers, but what of the other four? A look at the technology is worthwhile because it gives us an insight into the drive for bigger and better applications based on bigger and better technology. However, it also gives an insight into the limitations placed by the technology itself. Often software developers' dreams are thwarted by technology lagging behind their expectations, both of which are normally far in excess of a manager's perceived desires and needs.

Since the turn of the century we have been able to control electricity using valves and other thermionic devices. Putting large numbers of these valves together gave the first generation of computers, which were very large, expensive, prone to overheating and unreliable. Because of their size, cost and limited usefulness these machines were few and far between, normally being housed in universities or research departments of large organisations. Applications were limited to simple number crunching with little processing power and little available memory.

In the early 1950s, the development of the solid state transistor and other devices such as diodes and triodes gave rise to the second generation of computers. Whilst the early second generation computers had limited processing power they could access masses of memory using magnetic tape, thus making them ideal for repetitive tasks such as calculating the pay (a simple task) for hundreds of employees (which requires masses of memory). Most large organisations bought a computer to handle such things as accounts and payroll. These computers were large, expensive and required a well controlled environment. For these reasons they were installed centrally. Responsibilty and control were held by a data processing manager and his staff. Computing power was not available to the masses.

In the late 1950s, John F. Kennedy said that the Americans would have a man on the moon within ten years. To achieve this objective NASA needed to develop not just rocket technology but also advanced communication and navigation systems. Early science fiction films may have predicted rockets, space suits and space helmets but what they missed completely was the enormous amount of technology surrounding the astronauts in their capsule. The space programme gave the impetus to develop the third generation of computers based on LSIs or large-scale integrated circuits. These LSIs, known as silicon chips, could contain thousands of transistor equivalents. Outside the space programme, computer developers were not slow to realise that these chips could be used to produce computers that were cheap and powerful. Thus we move into the third generation of computers which are smaller, cheaper and more powerful than anything imagined twenty years before. This extended power was used to develop the early artificial intelligence applications, but such systems were still centrally held and controlled. Other than university installations which were developing research applications, computers were still in the hands of data processing specialists. Meanwhile, accountants and some managers were starting to use desk top calculators. These calculators were originally limited in scope with little processing power and less memory. As computers got smaller and more powerful the question was asked: is it not possible to get computing power on the manager's desk?

The move toward VLSIs, or very large-scale integrated circuits, gave the necessary processing power to build personal computers as part of the fourth generation. These computers are small, powerful and cheap.

Because they require no special environment they can be used on desk tops, in homes or in remote locations such as warehouses, shop floors and check out points in supermarkets. The development of small computers has been paralleled with an increase in the number of applications available to run on such machines. These include text processing, spreadsheets, databases, graphics, desk top publishing and, of course, small scale expert systems. No longer are these computers bought, run, programmed and controlled by data processing managers. Now they are literally in the hands of the user.

The initial computers were not very powerful. Applications were small scale. However, two things are happening. Firstly, personal computers are becoming more and more powerful so they are able to run languages that require large amounts of memory, such as PROLOG. The use of disks for memory storage means virtually instant access to very large quantities of data. Personal computers are now able to run fairly large packages, for example, expert systems, which have a real part to play in an organisation. Secondly, personal computers are being linked together in networks to create the ability for managers to talk to each other and also to communicate with a central computer which could hold an extremely large expert system.

The development of technology has seen subtle changes in the way computer systems are implemented in organisations. Originally they were highly centralised and dedicated to one or two main activities such as payrolls. The advancements in technology have meant small, cheap, powerful computers available on the desk top. It has been argued that if Rolls Royce cars had developed in the same way as computers they would do 500 mph, 1000 miles to the gallon, cost £5 and fit in a match box (Author's note: I am not sure who would want one). Nonetheless, this increasing power and decreasing cost has lead to decentralisation of computing resources. Managers are more aware of their possible application. The wheel has turned almost full circle with the power going back into the centre but with the peripheral users able to have their own computer linked to the centre. The large, central computer holds an enormous amount of information which can be accessed by users. Such information could be corporate data or even an expert system.

WHAT IS AN EXPERT SYSTEM?

An expert system is part of the larger domain of artificial intelligence. Despite the marketing propaganda they are not all powerful, magic replacements for humans. They are software packages designed to run on computers. Like all software packages they have their limitations as well as their benefits.

Most software is written in the form of an algorithm, which is a list of commands for the computer to carry out in the order prescribed. The algorithm will use data held in a separate file, which is stored in a particular way. Generally software can be considered as data + algorithm. Thus a payroll program will: look up the first person in the data, read his gross salary, deduct his tax allowance, evaluate the tax to be paid, deduct all other contributions such as superannuation, pension, trade union fees and produce the net pay. All of this will be printed in a defined way on the payslip. Having completed the first employee the payroll system will continue to evaluate the pay for all employees, be there one hundred or one thousand. The algorithm will not change for each employee.

Systems such as these are clearly based on early computer technology that was designed to carry out boring, repetitive numerical tasks. Subsequent applications reflect the changes in technology. The advent of personal computers has lead to smaller versions of payrolls based on spreadsheets, that is rows and columns of figures manipulated by the computer. Subsequently, computers have handled text in the form of word processing. The largest selling software has been spreadsheets and word processing packages.

However, managers handle more than words and numbers. They handle information. This leads to the development of databases, that is large stores of information stored in a structured way so that a manager could extract information as and when required. An example of a database would be an employee database where each employee would have a record and each record would contain relevant information such as name, address, date of birth, salary, department, etc. The manager could carry out analysis of his employees whenever necessary by interrogating the database, using an enquiry language, with questions like: list all the employees earning more than £10 000, with more than three years service and living within a particular area. The ability to interrogate the database is limited only by the information held and the need to conform to an enquiry language.

However, the manager is concerned not just with information but with knowledge. Information is data put together in a meaningful way. Knowledge is information interpreted for a particular application. Personal computer-based expert systems are designed to accumulate, store, interrogate and access such knowledge.

THE STRUCTURE OF EXPERT SYSTEMS

'An expert system is regarded as the embodiment within a computer of a knowledge-based component, from an expert skill, in such a form that the system can offer intelligent advice or take an intelligent decision about a processing function. A desirable additional characteristic, which many would consider fundamental, is the capability of the system, on demand, to justify its own line of reasoning in a manner directly intelligible to the enquirer. The style adopted to attain these characteristics is rule-based programming.' (British Computer Society.) Simply, an expert system can be considered as four components, see Figure 2.

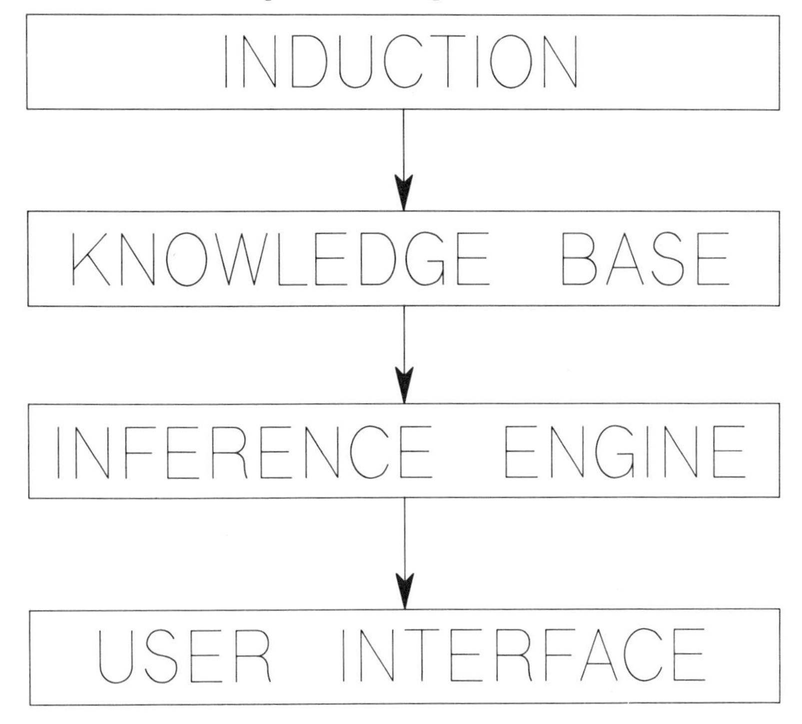

Figure 2: *The Components of an Expert System*

INDUCTION OF KNOWLEDGE

The first thing the potential user must do is put the 'knowledge' into the system. There are several ways of doing this depending on the level of sophistication of the expert system. If the expert system is 'rule-based', the knowledge can be entered as a set of rules. Alternatively, if the expert system is 'rule-inducing' the rules can be evaluated from existing data. For example, if you have a lot of data stored on a computer, such as a personnel record system, certain packages can access this information directly. This approach will be discussed in more detail later. Entering knowledge is not as easy as it would first appear. The system needs a coherent, comprehensive set of rules which cover all contingencies. Some of the inherent problems are discussed later.

KNOWLEDGE BASE

The knowledge base or rules is the heart of the system. Once entered the base will remain unchanged during operation of the system. This means that the user will access the knowledge base by interrogating the rules but the rules will not be changed. There will be occasions when the rules are updated, amended or added to, but these changes are separate to the normal interaction with the knowledge base.

INFERENCE ENGINE

The inference engine as the name implies is the part of the system that generates the answers. The engine accesses the rules and makes the necessary connections and conclusions. The type or number of rules does not affect the way the inference engine carries out its task. Thus it is possible to change the rules when necessary without affecting the inference engine although the inferences, that is, the path through the knowledge base, may change.

HUMAN INTERFACE

It is important that any system should be easy to use. Any errors should be spotted and help provided when required. An expert system has inbuilt help facilities as part of the interface with the user.

CHARACTERISTICS OF EXPERT SYSTEMS

An expert system running on a personal computer will have a set of characteristics that distinguish it from traditional computer applications:

ONE AREA OF KNOWLEDGE

An expert system will relate to one particular area of expertise or knowledge rather than a set of data.

ONE PARTICULAR PURPOSE

It will be constructed for a particular purpose such as giving advice on a particular topic.

RULES

Knowledge will usually be in the form of rules. It can be argued that human knowledge is collected together in the form of heuristics or rules.

INFERENCE

Knowledge and inference are separate. Buying an expert system shell will give the user the inference engine, an application will still require a knowledge base. An inference engine can be used in association with any knowledge base.

EXTENDABLE

Knowledge can be extended. The knowledge can start off fairly small and can be enlarged in a controlled way. It is possible to add related knowledge bases together.

HANDLE UNCERTAINTY

It may be that we are uncertain about the world. We cannot be certain that events are absolutely true or events are definitely going to happen. An expert system allows us to cope with these uncertainties.

GIVES ADVICE

The underlying rationale of an expert system is that it replaces an expert. Consequently, expert systems are specifically constructed to give advice rather than answers. Of course, the advice may be positive, for example, a system might give the advice 'you should go to Blackpool for your holiday'.

EXPLANATION

It can explain its reasoning. Because an expert system is designed to give advice to non-experts, a help facility is inbuilt. At any time during an interrogation of a system the user can ask for an explanation of why the system is following a particular train of thought, rather like asking a chess champion to explain his or her moves.

Thus, an expert system can be seen as:

System = Knowledge + Inference

Traditional programs are algorithms that manipulate data. As described earlier, this works well with repetitive tasks, thus

Program = Algorithm + Data

The data would consist of employee salaries and the algorithm would work out gross pay, net pay and tax for all employees. An expert system does not tread the same path. Its route through the knowledge base will be determined by the users responses during the interrogative use of the system.

It is possible to summarise the differences between expert systems and more traditional packages:

Traditional Package	Expert System
handles data	handles knowledge
uses algorithms	uses heuristics or rules
goes through repetitive process	goes through inferential process
based on large data bases	based on knowledge bases

There is one aspect of expert systems yet to be defined. The term expert system is used to describe both the facility for developing an application and the applications themselves. There are expert system shells, which are available packages, that enable users to develop applications. For example, an expert system shell may be used to generate an application that will give advice about personal taxation. This book is about developing applications but, of necessity, will talk about the different types of shells available.

WHY MANAGERS SHOULD CONSIDER THEM

Before looking at expert systems it may be worthwhile to consider briefly what do managers do? Whilst each manager is different and only you know what you actually spend your time doing, it is possible to make some general observations. Managers spend some of their time taking in information from the outside world in the form of memos, letters, etc. They spend some of their time producing information and relaying it to the outside world in the form of memos, letters, etc. In between the input and output is some thought process, often referred to as 'decision making' although such a term gives the process rather more credibility than it deserves. Often managers are not involved in rational, scientific decision making but are responding to day to day pressures of work and making snap judgements about matters which range from trivial to potentially catastrophic.

Primarily managers should consider using expert systems because they are an aid to decision making. Expert systems are concerned with knowledge not data. Rather than storing bits of information such as date of birth, salary, job title, etc the knowledge base of an expert system contains just that which is suggested: the knowledge of an expert. Thus the years of learning, experience and application embodied in an individual's knowledge can be encapsulated in a computer. This knowledge can be accessed quickly and easily by a manager to improve the quality of decision making. But why put the knowledge into an expert system? There are advantages in storing the knowledge in a computer rather than in a human:

—The knowledge is permanent and will not fade with age.

—It is easy to transfer the knowledge to any number of users provided they have a compatible computer.

—Generating a knowledge base imposes a structure on the experts who may not be well organised.

—This in turn means that the knowledge can be documented.

—The expert system application should be consistently right. However, it can be consistently wrong, but more of that later.

—Finally, the difference between humans and expert systems is one of cost. An expert, senior consultant, senior partner, whatever label you choose will be a rare commodity. This has two ramifications. Firstly, they are always either in the wrong place, the other office, on leave or ill, or dead. Secondly, they are expensive. Encapsulating their knowledge in an expert system is both desirable, because it can be used at any time, and affordable, because of the drastic reductions in the cost of computing power and the availability of suitable software packages.

What can these knowledge bases be used for within an organisation?

—They can be used as a way of preserving knowledge so that when the expert retires, dies or leaves, the knowledge is still there.

—As knowledge grows within the organisation it may well outstrip individuals, or the amount of information at one time may be excessive, for example, monitoring data from an off-shore oil rig.

—An expert system can be used as a way of disseminating information around the organisation.

—It becomes possible for employees further down the knowledge tree (and down the payscale) to use the knowledge base to free the time of the expert. The degree of use will vary according to the circumstances. A car mechanic may let a receptionist use a knowledge base to give estimates to customers about the length and costs of car repairs, but a consultant surgeon may not want his receptionist using a knowledge base to diagnose patients in his absence.

—Expert systems can be used as part of training systems, especially when linked with interactive video. Because an expert system disseminates information, it can be used to create new experts by passing on skills from one generation to the next. This use of computer assisted instruction means that the wheel does not have to be re-invented and future generations can add to the knowledge base rather than spending long periods trying to learn it.

GETTING STARTED

Expert system shells are like any other software package in that there are fairly clear guidelines to follow. The prospective user should:

—gain some understanding of the software by talking to colleagues, reading relevant journals and reading a good book.

—buy a package and the hardware if it is not already available.

—choose a suitable area of application, develop the rules and interrogate the system.

—build bigger and better systems.

It is likely that a manager will entrust the development of a large system to somebody with knowledge and experience in building large systems, but he or she must have an understanding of how the system was built and its limitations. The difference between expert systems and other business software, such as spreadsheets and databases, is how they work, not how the package should be chosen and implemented. The process can follow the usual stages of implementing software mentioned above. All of these stages will be covered in the following chapters.

SUMMARY

The advent of smaller, more powerful computers has led to the development of new types of software for use by managers. An example of this new breed of applications is expert systems. This chapter opened with an introduction to expert systems, what they are and where they came from. It continued with definitions of the relevant terms used when discussing expert systems, discussing in some detail the component parts of an expert system. Then it reviewed the benefits of expert systems to managers, showing the necessary stages of implementation.

2

Aspects of Expert Systems

INTRODUCTION

In the first chapter we looked at the component parts of an expert system. These are the parts provided by the shell, but the end user is concerned with applications and not the shell itself. The term 'end user', often used in computing, refers to the person at the end of the software chain: developer–manufacturer–seller–buyer–user. An application is the knowledge base in a particular domain or area of expertise. Whilst the quality of the user interface is important and will vary with each particular shell, the quality of the knowledge base is the ultimate determinant of the usefulness and effectiveness of the application. As stated earlier the knowledge base is a set of rules. This is not true for all expert systems, but is generally true and to consider alternatives at this stage would be confusing. Should one consider using an existing expert system or developing an application first? It is probably better to get an idea of where you are going before talking in detail about how to get there. This chapter will look in detail at aspects of expert systems, before discussing how to build one in the next chapter. Firstly, we need to consider the concept of rules.

WHAT IS A KNOWLEDGE BASE?

How do humans know things? Simply, we store lots of facts which are sometimes relevant to the situation in which we find ourselves. That raises the next question. How do we know which facts are relevant and how do we apply them? A simple view of human memory is that it consists of a large collection of boxes, each with a label and contents. Thus we have a box labelled 'schooldays' and everything about our schooldays are kept under that heading. However, this model has an inherent flaw. It may be that thoughts or conversation about one topic such as meals or in particular rice pudding will trigger thoughts about school meals, in particular school rice pudding. It would appear that any area of our memory will trigger any other area as long as there is a connection, however tenuous. A more sophisticated model, or at least a suggestion, is that our memory is an enormous collection of information or knowledge. Not only do we have knowledge but we have knowledge about our knowledge. What we know, 'surface knowledge', is structured and organised. We know how the knowledge is structured. This know-how is known as deep knowledge.

Bits of information are important, but it is the relationships between them which are important. Such relationships can be stored in the form of rules called heuristics, a Greek term used to describe a method of education whereby students discover for themselves the answers to problems. It is now used to describe the way knowledge or ideas are linked, for example, we have weather folklore such as 'red sky at night, shepherd's delight'.

Whilst we can consider the human memory as a set of heuristics which are difficult to define and identify, we need to be more precise when creating knowledge to be used as the knowledge base in an expert system. Such knowledge will be stored as clearly defined rules. A rule is normally entered and stored in a knowledge base in the form:

if... then...

This is a condition–action pair, which means that if the first condition is satisfied the action is implemented, or 'fired'. Examples of rules are:

if it is raining
then I will take an umbrella

if he is an engineer
then he will earn 10 000

if temperature is greater than 250 degrees
then shut down reactor

Conditions can take a variety of forms including statements, such as 'it is raining', numerical comparisons, including = <> < > <= >=, and conditions can be applied to direct inputs from the outside world, such as pressure and temperature readings from gauges of a chemical production plant. Conditions can be multiples joined by 'and' or 'or', for example:

> if the sun is shining and the birds are singing
> or the leaves are falling

Actions or outcomes can be statements, commands or triggers to control the outside world such as process control. Any statement can be used to fire another rule.

In addition to the condition–action pair each rule is likely to have two further parts. Firstly, it should have a rule label. This label can range from a simple tag, for example, R1, to a full explanatory label, for example, 'Taking Umbrella Rule'. Keeping track of rules is straightforward in a small knowledge base with ten rules but becomes increasingly difficult as the knowledge base grows. Some packages, listed in Chapter seven, have rule dictionaries, that enable users to cross reference rules, so that they can navigate their way around the data. To give some indication of size, a demonstration system would be, say, 50 rules. A working system might be 1000 rules. A large system, the knowledge of an expert, might be 10 000 rules, and, it is estimated, a human stores anything up to 100 000 rules or heuristics. Although systems can be very large, a working system of great benefit to the organisation might only be 50 rules. Nonetheless it is still necessary to label rules clearly and keep track of them. Labelling and dictionaries will be covered in more detail in Chapter five.

One of the differences between expert systems and traditional programs is the level of explanation. An early payroll system will go through all employees pay without giving the user any help whatsoever. In fact the system was designed to be autonomous so it would run effortlessly and without stopping. More recent packages have inbuilt help facilities. However, these tend to give you help with the commands you have available rather than giving you some explanation of what they are doing and why. Expert systems can, to a certain extent, explain their behaviour but the explanation must be built into the system. Current expert systems cannot create their own help based on the rules in the knowledge base. This facility may be a feature of future systems. Meanwhile, the second addition to the rule is a statement of explanation. This explanation will be discussed in more detail later, in Chapter four. An example of a complete rule would be:

label	R26 Taking Umbrella
condition	If (it is raining)
action	Then (take an umbrella)
explanation	Because it will stop you getting wet

You may feel that the world cannot be described simply as a set of rules. Nonetheless, generally, expertise can be embodied in rules. A considerable amount of our human activities can be considered as heuristics or rules and can be embodied in an expert system knowledge base. The 'intelligence' of an expert system is the way in which the inference engine links the rules together. Whether or not it is worth the effort of setting up a system we will consider later in Chapter three.

THE INFERENCE ENGINE

FORWARD vs BACKWARD CHAINING

An expert system is a set of rules contained in a knowledge base that is accessed through some interface. This does not explain how the rules are linked. The example of the umbrella quoted above is useful enough if it is raining, but a knowledge domain with one or two rules hardly requires an expert system. However, when you have ten, a hundred or a thousand rules then the complexity increases. Not only are there more rules but also there are likely to be more and more connections between them. To extend our weather example there may be several rules relating to rain:

R26 If (it is raining)
then (take an umbrella)

R34 If (it is cloudy and the path is wet)
then (it is raining)

R43 If (the sky is grey)
then (it is cloudy)

R67 If (take an umbrella)
then (leave umbrella on train)

R88 If (leave footprints)
then (the path is wet)

The inference engine will make sense of these rules and link them together to ask the right questions to establish the correct conclusions. But which are the questions and which are conclusions? This set of rules can be used for two purposes. It can be used to ascertain whether or not one needs an umbrella. It will start with the question 'Is the sky grey?' in rule 43 which will fire rule 88 which will ask 'Do you leave footprints?'. This will fire 34 then 26 then 67. The outcome to the interrogation of the rules will be 'you will leave your umbrella on the train'.

Conversely, we might want to ask what are the conditions that led up to leaving the umbrella on the train. The inference engine will trace back from rule 67 to 26, then to 34, then to 43 and 88, and in response to the question 'Why did I leave my umbrella on the train?' will reply 'Because you leave footprints and the sky is grey'. Whilst this example appears ludicrous it serves to distinguish between forward and backward chaining systems. Forward chaining involves asking questions, establishing answers that are added to the working memory, and the rules run through again using these answers; for example, if rule 43 is fired then we have the fact that it is cloudy. Forward chaining, sometimes called data-driven, is illustrated by the first use of the umbrella knowledge base.

Backward chaining, also known as goal-driven, as the name suggests involves identifying conclusions and tracking back to see from whence they came and is illustrated by the second use of the umbrella knowledge base. The two approaches both have advantages and disadvantages in different contexts. If the number of possible outcomes are known and small then backward chaining is very efficient. Conversely, if the number of outcomes is large then forward chaining is preferable. Most expert systems tend to be backward chaining because the outcome is known and the factors leading up to the outcome are required, for example, a medical researcher may want to establish the contributory factors to lung cancer.

DEPTH vs BREADTH

A knowledge base will have two dimensions. This makes it possible to go not only forwards or backwards (as in forward or backward chaining) but also to go sideways, that is, look at rules that are at the same level in the knowledge base. If the system is very large it may not be possible for the user to complete a full search of the knowledge base because of time constraints, or, more likely, restrictions on computer power. Thus the search is non-exhaustive, that is, does not examine all possibilities. It is likely that the inference engine will search depth first. It will start at the opening question and go through the rules until a solution is reached, assuming a forward chaining system. This may not be the best solution. Had the inference engine pursued a different line of enquiry then there may be a different solution. Most packages are depth first, although more sophisticated inference engines allow the user to determine the method of enquiry.

To illustrate the difference in the two approaches, imagine a specialist versus a generalist. The former will ask more and more detailed questions until satisfied that the problem has been solved. The latter will leap around asking apparently irrelevant questions until the problem is solved. It is the lilypad versus the microscope approach. In a small system where it is possible to search all rules, then methods of cutting down the search become irrelevant, although any mechanism that reduces search time without losing optimal solutions should not be discounted. One such approach, which allows an experienced user to restrict the search pattern, is to allow the user to give information to the system without prompting. Such information can obviate the need for large groups of rules to be used. As an example, let us assume we are interrogating a knowledge base about our proposed summer holiday. We know that the system will eventually ask if we want sunshine. We can avoid all the rules relating to the weather if we specify at the outset that the climate is irrelevant to our needs.

INTERROGATING A SYSTEM

Having created a set of rules using the generator provided by the package, how would a user interrogate the system?

SWITCH ON

The first thing the user will notice, if using a reasonable system, is that the system is unlike any previous computer software. It will use colour graphics and other devices to make the screen interesting, friendly and useful. There are three factors that allow expert systems to work in this way. Firstly, expert systems are almost state of the art, in other words they use the most up-to-date ideas and technology. Therefore, they must look better than packages based on ideas of the sixties and seventies. Secondly, people generating expert systems' shells and applications have an interest in all aspects of artificial intelligence. They tend to be conscious of the human element of systems since it is humans they are trying to replicate. Thirdly, the very nature of expert systems should give them a friendly interactive interface with the user.

If the system is a dedicated system to one application then the system will automatically start up, otherwise the user will have to choose an application from a menu of choices. Systems vary in the ease with which users can select applications. Some will give a full listing of available applications with a pointer on the screen that the user can move around. Others, less sophisticated, will expect the user to type in a list of commands.

STATE OBJECTIVE

Having chosen an application, the user may be asked to specify their objective in using the system. This serves two purposes. Firstly, the inference engine will use that part of the knowledge base that relates directly to the user's problem. For example, the user may want to interrogate a system that will help them choose a holiday. They could be asked to specify home or abroad which will access different sets of rules although the inference engine will work in the same way on both.

If the system is capable of forward and backward chaining, the user will be asked which inference method they wish to use. The user could ask which holiday will satisfy a set of conditions, for example, endless sunshine and beaches, conversely, the user could ask if they choose Barbados which conditions will it give them?

ANSWER QUESTIONS

Having chosen an area of expertise and the way the user wishes to use the knowledge base, they will be asked a series of questions taken from the rules. Each answer will temporarily change the knowledge and trigger or fire further questions depending on the previous answers. As each question is answered so the inference engine will pass through the rules to see if any are now relevant. Returning to our holiday example, the first question may be:

'Do you like outdoor holidays?'

Answering yes to this question will add to the knowledge held in the computer. The inference engine will search through the rule base and ask a series of question developing the theme of outdoor holidays.

Answering no to this question will prompt the inference engine to pursue different lines of enquiry which will invoke different questions, based on other rules, for example:

Answering YES may trigger the question:

> 'Do you like sport?'

Answering NO may trigger the question:

> 'Do you like painting or drawing?'

Responding YES or NO to the next question will invoke further questions until the inference engine has completed its excursion through the knowledge base. Such a series of questions and answers may give the feeling that there is a set algorithm that is being followed by the computer, but this is not the case. The questions asked by the system are based on rules which are triggered by the user's answers to other rules. At any point during the interaction, the user can invoke a help facility to ask why the computer is asking particular questions. The level of help will vary between packages. Such help is discussed in more detail in Chapter three.

REITERATE

The system will run through the data until a conclusion is reached. The user will then be given various options. They will be allowed to change answers to see different outcomes, they will be allowed to restart the system with a completely new set of answers or they will be given the option of starting a different knowledge base.

THE BENFITS OF EXPERT SYSTEMS

Having looked at an expert system in some detail we can consider the benefits of such an approach compared with traditional programming:

REPRESENTATION OF KNOWLEDGE

Early applications for computers used languages that manipulated numbers. Consequently, the applications themselves were about numbers, such as payroll systems, numerical analysis, etc., suitable for engineering, sciences and accounting. As computing technology improved and became cheaper and more powerful, so computers handled text as well as numbers, and data systems using information such as text processors and databases were introduced. The next development was the storage, assimilation and retrieval of knowledge, in the form of expert systems, defined as 'a computer program that gives expert advice'. Whilst not suggesting that expert systems are going to replace humans entirely, or even just their brain, we do see a different approach to computing that we have not seen before.

TRANSPARENCY

Anybody using a traditional package will know very little about the program if it were written by someone else. This is true for the word processing package I am using for this book. I press a button and something happens. Likewise it is true for other applications you may use. Your accountant could provide you with a program to analyse your projected cash flow during the next twelve months. If you change your thoughts on revenue or expenditure then you change the numbers and the bottom line changes. You may not know how or, even worse, why the changes have occurred in the way they did on your bottom line. Only the person creating the package fully understands the way it works and the underlying assumptions.

It is argued that expert systems are transparent, by which is meant the internal workings of the system are more obvious to the user. The program is no longer a black box with the user putting in a number at one end and the answer coming out at the other. The assumptions underlying the expert system application should be more explicit so the user knows why the system is working like it is. This is helped by the level of explanation available. As the user interrogates the system, an interactive rapport is built up between user and system. This allows the user to feel more comfortable using the system. If any problems arise then the user can ask for help or explanation. The system should also be able to retrace its steps through the knowledge base and explain how it reached a particular question.

Knowing the assumptions and being able to ask for explanation increases the user's understanding of the system. In turn this understanding leads to more faith in the system matched with increased confidence in using the system. The often quoted term 'user friendly' becomes meaningful. In the past, 'user friendly' did not mean making the system transparent so the user knew what they were doing. Rather, it meant the system patronised the user by making the instructions as simple as possible. An expert system should be simple to use, but how it works should also be understood by the user.

Because they are fully interactive with an emphasis on true friendliness, expert systems are ideal vehicles for generating training systems where the trainees can learn by experience without being confused, threatened or feeling they are being lead by a black box.

VERSATILE

Traditional applications were analysed by an analyst, designed by a designer, programmed by a programmer and used by a user. This appears to be a neat straightforward state of affairs but in practice it made life very difficult. There were so many links in such a system that the user was never really part of the development process. Any changes to the system would require major rewrites of the software with possible implications for other parts of the system. As the system grew, so the application would try to keep in touch. Expert systems are more versatile, they can start small with a particular area of knowledge (knowledge domain) and grow as time allows. Not only can a knowledge base grow but such bases can be merged, so the knowledge in one area can be linked to the knowledge of another, for example, knowledge about product A can be combined with knowledge about product B, although this may place the expert system outside the scope of an individual. Since the knowledge is a set of rules which can be of any size, the expansion is theoretically endless. The inference engine copes with more and more rules because whatever you do to the rules the inference engine remains unchanged.

Not only can the rules grow but the rules can be changed easily. Thus changes in knowledge can be incorporated easily into the system. No longer does the program have to be rewritten, a dangerous and difficult task because traditional programs are notoriously undecipherable to subsequent readers. Any changes to particular rules need not affect other parts of the system as we shall see later.

It is evident that expert systems are different to traditional programming methods. There is an inbuilt friendliness both for the developer and the subsequent user which is lacking in most other applications. This gives rise to more confidence, and more versatility.

THE LIMITATIONS OF EXPERT SYSTEMS

Having said that expert systems are different, why are they not widespread? Clearly, any approach has limitations and expert systems are no exception. The development in computer hardware and software is running faster than the market place can cope. It is often said that expert systems are a solution looking for a problem and this contains a grain of truth. Expert systems arise from work done on programming languages and AI applications rather than a solution to a particular problem. Consequently they are available but not readily taken up by end users.

Expert systems are still in a stage of development . The quality of shells available now is much improved on the shells available only twelve months ago. It remains to be seen whether expert systems are part of an evolution or the start of a new dawn in computing.

Some of the limitations that restrain expert systems in organisations and which will preclude their development are given below.

OBSERVATIONS AT A GIVEN TIME

Although any system may take considerable time to develop, this time will be comparatively short compared with the length of time the system will be in use. If this is not true then why spend so much time developing the system? However, the system will be a reflection of knowledge at a particular time. Clearly, there is opportunity to update the knowledge base if it has been well constructed and documented, but the model will remain for the life of the system. Any knowledge base must be constructed to fit the expert system shell and this leads to a particular view of the world. This view may be appropriate today but not tomorrow. Suppose we have a medical system that helps diagnose dyspepsia, we will construct it using available rules but we may change our views about dyspepsia. Suppose we discover that stomach upsets are caused by ill-fitting shoes, we would need a major rethink of the model. If you think such a change is unlikely remember that major advances in the health of a population are caused by clean water and good sanitation, factors outside the medical profession. Similarly, we may create a marketing model and then change our view of our markets. We may want to develop a completely new marketing strategy for the third world for example.

CONSTANT WAY TO SOLVE PROBLEMS

Linked to the first limitation is the inbuilt notion that there is a consistent way to solve problems which is embodied in the expert system. The means of solving the problem may be self-evident today but may be less obvious tomorrow. On a large scale we have had transitions from stone to iron age or pre- and post-industrial revolution. On a smaller scale, the introduction of microtechnology in washing machines has removed the need for electromechanical parts that were unreliable and untrustworthy. At least using an expert system gives the advantage that an application is easier to update and change because of the way it is constructed.

ASSUMES SAME FOR ALL EXPERTS

Using an expert to create a set of rules assumes that the expert knows all the rules. Further, it assumes that there is agreement about the rules. In other words it does not matter which expert is chosen as all experts will create the same rule base. This is unlikely. Mentioning pains in your stomach to a surgeon may result in him removing your appendix. The same complaint to your general practitioner may result in you being given a bottle of indigestion tablets. It may be that there is broad agreement between experts but reaching total agreement is difficult if not impossible. Recognising the problem of integrating different views has been acknowledged by researchers who are developing techniques for combining experts' knowledge using a variety of techniques such as 'blackboarding', that is, writing up views and attempting to reconcile them prior to incorporating the rule into the knowledge base, see Chapter three.

ASSUMES BEST APPROACH

The concept of an expert system assumes that a best, or at least a viable, solution is available. However, it is conceivable that certain problems are insurmountable and unanswerable at least with our present state of knowledge. In such cases the expert system should not give an answer. Furthermore, it is possible that the solution offered by the expert system is not available. An expert system may suggest lowering the river rather than raising the bridge. What happens to the credibility of the system? Alternatively, the solution offered may be available but it may be unacceptable to the user. Any system must be responsive to the particular views of the user. This responsiveness is discussed in Chapter four.

POLITICS

An expert system assumes a perfect world which we do not have as yet. Any use of an expert system must be within the normal constraints of decision making in organisations. Organisational decisions are often sufficing rather than optimising. That is to say such decisions provide a satisfactory solution to the problem rather than provide the best, that is, optimal solution. The reason why we suffice rather than optimise is because we always work with limited resources. We are short of time, money, information, equipment or the necessary manpower to provide an optimal solution. We get by. Will we be able to cope with expert systems that give us perfect information and advice? Furthermore, there are political influences both on the decision processes and the outcomes. Any solution will not necessarily satisfy all the people all the time. Can an expert system attempting to replicate the real world cope with the politics of decision making in organisations? For the moment, humans will use the advice given by expert systems as part of the political process rather than relying entirely on any advice given. In the future we may need to be more aware of the apolitical nature of expert systems or at least aware of the politics of the expert whose knowledge is embodied in the knowledge base.

SUMMARY

This chapter has explored in more detail the various aspects of expert systems. It started with a look at rules, what they are and how they are constructed. Having established the basis of an expert system, it went on to look at how a system would be interrogated by a user. Having a better understanding of what they are and how they work, it examined the benefits of expert systems in more detail. Finally it looked at some of the limitations of expert systems in organisations. These limitations tend to be limitations of the organisation rather than limitations of the software.

3
Choosing an Application

INTRODUCTION

An expert system is a body of knowledge, embodied in a set of rules, that can be accessed and interrogated by a non-expert. Implicit in this definition is the assumption that within organisations are bodies of knowledge worth building into an expert system. However, not all knowledge or sets of knowledge are worth the time and effort required to convert them into the rules of a knowledge base. This chapter will consider the factors that influence whether or not it is worth the effort. Of course, one useful indication of likely success is knowing that somebody has taken the time to develop a system similar to one you have in mind. Chapter seven gives examples of working systems, both large and small, and indicates likely areas of possible success. Bear in mind that your applications will be determined by your needs and not just past experience.

IDENTIFYING AREAS OF EXPERTISE

One supplier of an expert system running on a personal computer suggested that organisations should create expert systems so that the expert need not be on hand all of the time. The implication being they could play golf, tennis or whatever whilst the workers back at the office or factory used the system. Essentially this is true. Any system should allow lots of people to access knowledge easily and quickly. Whether or not the expert then disappears to the golf course is a matter of individual or corporate conscience. Nonetheless the spirit is true. An expert system should transfer the knowledge of an expert or experts to a broader group. In what circumstances would this be advisable?

Firstly, the expert may be about to leave the company because of retirement or transfer. Such a person will have accumulated knowledge over a ten, twenty or thirty year period. Under this heading we could include death of the expert as an example of involuntary transfer. Rather than lose all the knowledge and expertise, the solution is to create an expert system. Secondly, the knowledge may be held by one person but may be required by many. In the case of a manufacturing company, detailed knowledge of the product may rest with the designers and production engineers but the people responsible for the product eventually are service mechanics and technicians. Creating a system embodying knowledge about the company's product will make life easier for the service engineer and more satisfactory for the customer. Thirdly, the knowledge base can grow to such an extent that an expert can no longer retain all the knowledge easily, giving rise to delays and errors. An example here would be a doctor with more and more case histories about certain illnesses or diseases who might lose track of the information. This excess of information could make diagnosis slow and possibly less than perfect. Similarly, the more complex production systems become, the more difficult it is to monitor them, detect breakdowns in the production process and decide on the necessary action to be taken. Two obvious examples here are oil rigs and nuclear reactors. Rigs are incredibly complex systems manned by a small staff, where the inability to detect and rectify faults can cost thousands; nuclear reactors are complex systems where mistakes can be cataclysmic.

CRITERIA FOR CHECKING POTENTIAL AREAS

When attempting to identify potential areas for developing applications it is necessary to consider if such applications are both feasible and desirable. An expert system, like any software, is desirable if it does one of two things. Either an expert system should be cost effective by increasing revenue or reducing costs or, alternatively, it should contribute to the efficiency of an organisation by providing expertise that otherwise would not be available.

Having determined that an application is desirable it is necessary to consider if an application is feasible. Criteria that can be used to determine feasibility are given below and are summarised in Figure 3. Of course, such criteria could themselves be embodied in an expert system application. In addition, each person or organisation may add parameters of success that are not listed, for example, an organisation may want to encapsulate knowledge only where there is an immediate threat of knowledge loss, or it may want to restrict the size of first attempts to small scale projects.

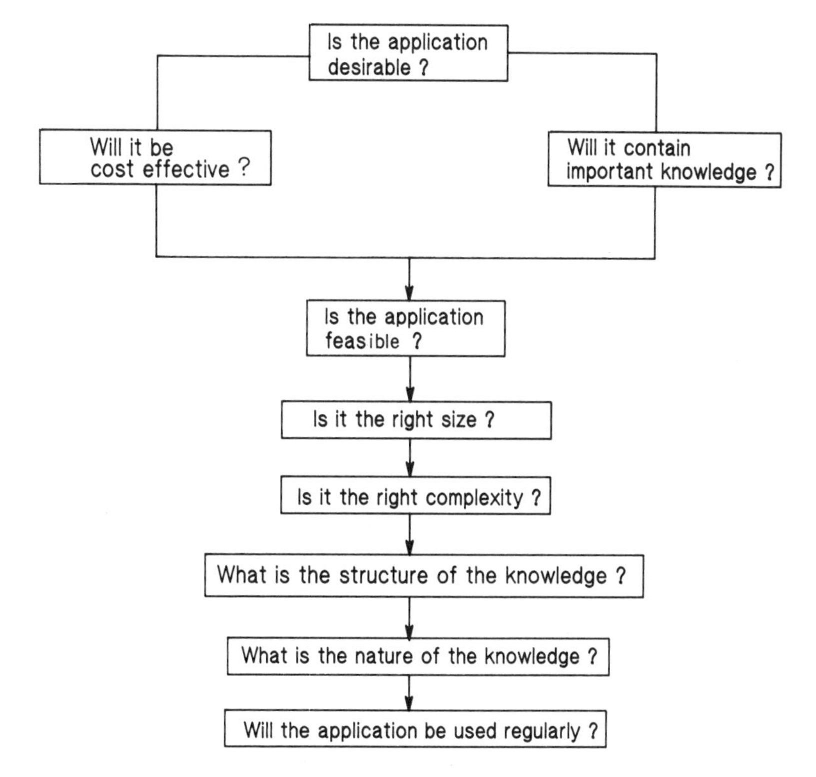

Figure 3: *Criteria for Evaluating Potential Applications*

SIZE AND COMPLEXITY

Do not consider projects where the outcome is trivial. It may well be that there is an elaborate expert system containing masses of knowledge within hundreds of rules, but if the outcome is silly then why bother? An example of this would be trying to encapsulate all the weather information in the world to determine whether or not to keep an umbrella in the boot of the car just in case of rain. Similarly, very small sets of knowledge do not require massive computer power to handle them, a rule that applies to all computer software applications. For example, if you need to determine which employee should be used for a particular project, this can be handled manually if you have only two employees.

Conversely, the size of expert systems being considered here, that is, systems running on a personal computer, will not allow massive systems to be developed. They will have limitations as to the number of rules they can handle, or, more likely, the larger they get the slower they become because the computer cannot handle them. It is a good idea to start with a manageable system so that you can keep track of rules and outcomes and thus make testing and running easier. This is discussed in more detail later.

CURRENT FORMULATION

Expert systems are not only a way of storing knowledge but should also be a way of gathering or collecting knowledge together. The better the package the more help it will be in gathering the information. More of this later, but at the moment just consider how the information exists at the present time. If it is well established, well structured and documented then it does not need an expert system to pull it together. For example, the highway code is simple, straightforward and easy to understand; so why bother to try and do anything to it. On the other hand, the information on your organisation about which customers buy what, and when, may be fragmented and unstructured. Such information is ripe for a tidying up process that would be a forerunner to an expert system.

REGULARITY OF USE

If I intend travelling abroad by car for my holidays I will go through an elaborate decision process based on a set of rules. The sorts of things I will consider are: which crossing, day or night, which port to which port, which car, which autoroute, which ferry company, etc. These questions can be answered using a set of clear rules, in fact, such an example is an excellent use of an expert system, except the time taken to generate the system will exceed the length of the holiday. If I were a tour operator or an automobile association with broader responsibilities to my members I may well consider the time taken to be worthwhile but as an individual who makes one crossing a year, the time taken to generate the system far exceeds the benefits.

Conversely, it is precisely the infrequent application that should prove the most benefit to individuals. Why should I spend the time working out a route manually when all the information is there for someone to create an expert system? The answer, of course, is the frequency of my use compared with the world at large. This has been recognised by some shell suppliers who will also sell applications. These applications are not cost effective for a single user to develop. However, they are ideal as centrally developed applications used only a few times by the buyer. Such expert system applications work rather like advice for consumers about products, for example, the various televisions on the market. A potential purchaser will only need this information once, but it is very useful if it is accessible when needed. Example applications are given in Chapter eleven.

NATURE OF THE INFORMATION

If the information involved in the decision process is purely numeric then a simple traditional computer algorithm will suffice. Not only will it be easier to construct, it will probably be faster and more robust. On the other hand, if the decisions involve the manipulation of ideas, linking them together to give complex linkings before a final outcome is determined, in other words, if the problem requires what can be considered as 'common sense', with a necessity to interrogate, augment and update the information, then an expert system is likely to be the solution. An expert system would also be useful when speed and accessibility are important, for example when interrogating a knowledge base containing DHSS regulations.

COST/BENEFIT ANALYSIS

Expert systems applications are created with the intention of replacing an expert or, at least, making the expert's knowledge more widely available. In itself this may be a perfectly reasonable objective, but is it worthwhile? To answer this question you should consider not what is the immediate aim, that is, to create a knowledge base, but what is the long term aim? What will an expert system do for your business?

BENEFITS

You are in business to provide goods or services in return for which you receive money. It may be that the money you receive is not revenue which gives profits but a budget within which you must operate. One of your aims in life is to increase profits or reduce costs.

Developing and implementing an expert system should help you do one or the other in one of three ways. Firstly, you can increase productivity. In other words, you do the same thing but more of it, given the resources available. Secondly, you can gain competitive advantage over your rivals. Such advantages can stem from reduced costs, improved product, better sales support, better after-sales service or more effective marketing. Thirdly, you can create new business opportunities. This may mean anything from marketing a new product, to a new market, to discovering an enormous new oilfield. Any proposed benefits should be tangible and measurable.

COSTS

The costs of an expert system can be considered under three parts: hardware, software and people. Hardware costs include not only the computer itself but also all the other incidental costs. Each of these costs may be small but they mount up. Items to consider here include the computer, printer, maintenance charges, paper, printer ribbons, disks, storage boxes for the disks, etc. Apparently insignificant items, such as a cable to connect the printer to the computer, can be quite expensive. Budget for your total requirements.

The second item, software, covers the initial cost of the expert system shell and any related software that you buy initially. Whilst you may hesitate to spend £2000 on an expert system shell when shells are available for £500, bear in mind that the subsequent costs may be considerably less. The inherent help and support in a £2000 package may pay for itself tenfold.

The third item, people, refers to the costs of training, developing and using a system. Whilst there will be some expenditure on material items, the largest cost will be salaries and overheads. This cost can be measured in units of time. Most software development projects talk of 'man days' or 'man years'. The longer the project, the more it costs. The cost of people should be doubled. You should consider each day spent on the project as one cost. However, you should also consider the opportunity cost, or rather the lost opportunity cost. Suppose your marketing manager is involved in creating a knowledge base of all he knows about marketing. Such a knowledge base will have long term benefits for your company, but at what cost? Each day spent working on the expert system is a day less spent marketing in Japan or wherever. Thus the time spent is doubled. The time actually spent on the project and the time lost elsewhere.

ESTIMATING

If you ask car manufacturers how long it takes to produce a car, they can tell you to the nearest minute. If you ask builders how long it takes to build a house, they can tell you to the nearest week, weather permitting. If you ask software developers how long it will take to develop a piece of software, they can tell you to the nearest year, give or take a twinge. Software projects are notoriously bad at creating and meeting deadlines. One survey suggested that 15% of software projects do not deliver anything and the remaining 85% are often late. Overruns of the order of 100–200% are common. Clearly, there is some need to improve the quality of software project management to bring it into line with engineering. How can we estimate the timescale of a project?

Imagine someone you know is going to have a baby. How tall will the baby be when it is fully grown? The first thing to do is look for historical or past evidence. How tall are the parents, siblings, other relatives? We note that males are taller than females on average. Next we can identify any cultural or environmental factors that may help. A Japanese person will be shorter than a Scandanavian person. Thirdly, we look for circumstances particular to this baby that will influence height. If the baby will be one of twins then it will be smaller at birth but should grow to its full height eventually. Similarly, running two projects concurrently will slow both down but they should both get there in the end. Using all the evidence available, past history, external influences, particular circumstances, we can make an estimate of the future size. In fact, we make two estimates, one for a boy and one for a girl. These estimates will have three components: accuracy, range and certainty. We can say with absolute certainty that the baby will grow to be five feet tall plus or minus three feet. We can be less certain that the eventual height will be five feet six inches plus or minus two inches. The notion of certainty or probability is discussed in more detail in Chapter four.

When the baby is born we will refine our estimate to the further evidence into account. Knowing the sex and size of the baby should help us be more accurate in our estimate or prediction. The range of the estimate should reduce and we should offer an opinion with more confidence or certainty. These changes are the fourth component of estimating: convergence. As the baby grows into a toddler, then a child and, finally, an adult, we can refine our estimate further and further. We can compare previous estimates with actual measurements to help us improve our final prediction. The success of our estimating is a function of convergence. We know that estimates improve over time. The faster our estimates improve, that is, converge on the actual, the better is our estimating, see Figure 4. The quality of our estimating is not the initial accuracy of the prediction but the reciprocal of the average discrepancy of our predictions. In other words, the closer our overall average prediction is to the actual timescale the better our estimating.

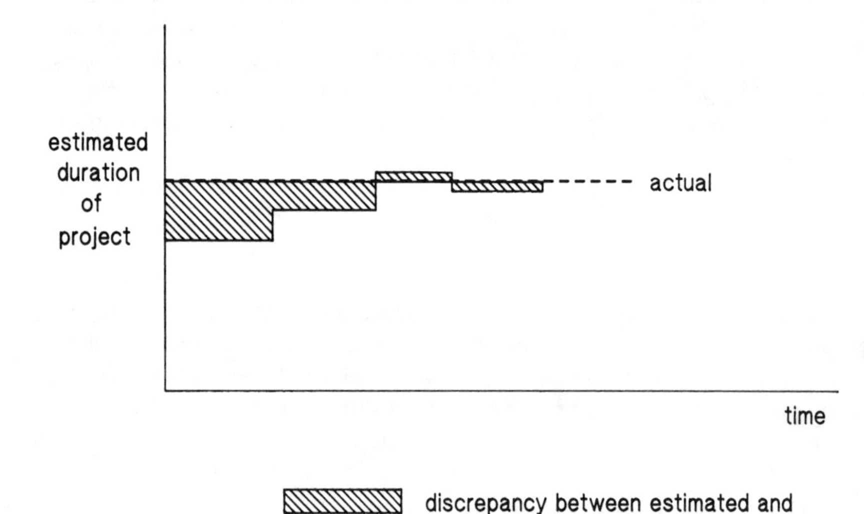

Figure 4: *The Convergence of Estimates*

Estimating the length of a project is not an exact science. We should accept that the first figure we arrive at is an estimate. However, this figure can and should be refined as the project progresses. Given the emotional involvement of the people developing the system, perhaps the estimation of time and related costs should be undertaken by a third party.

The eventual height of a baby is a relatively simple example because we have lots of past experience and statistical tables to help us make a prediction. Any software project is more difficult to estimate. To determine the time scale of such a project we can breakdown the project into more manageable parts. Developing an expert system application requires several smaller tasks to be undertaken: purchase shell, create and test rules, train users, write documentation, etc. Each of these tasks can form the basis of an estimate or be further subdivided into smaller tasks for estimation purposes. The level of task subdivision, known as granularity, is determined by the level of information we have. It is pointless subdividing 'create rules' into 'create rule 1', 'create rule 2', ... if we can be no more accurate about each rule than we are about the total knowledge base. Dividing the project into very small parts may only create unnecessary work and confusion without contributing to the initial accuracy of the time estimates. Of course, developing an expert system can be considered as project development and any of the software available for handling projects can be utilised.

MAN YEARS

A popular notion in software development is the 'man year', or, for smaller projects, the 'man month' or 'man day'. Thus someone selling a software product will proclaim 'it took ten man years to develop'. Does this mean one man for ten years or ten men for one year? You may recall from your schooldays the problems of three men digging a hole in four days .... There is an obvious solution to the time taken to develop software. If it is going to take one man ten years, then use ten men. It should only take one year. Unfortunately, man years are more myth than reality. As the number of people employed on an activity

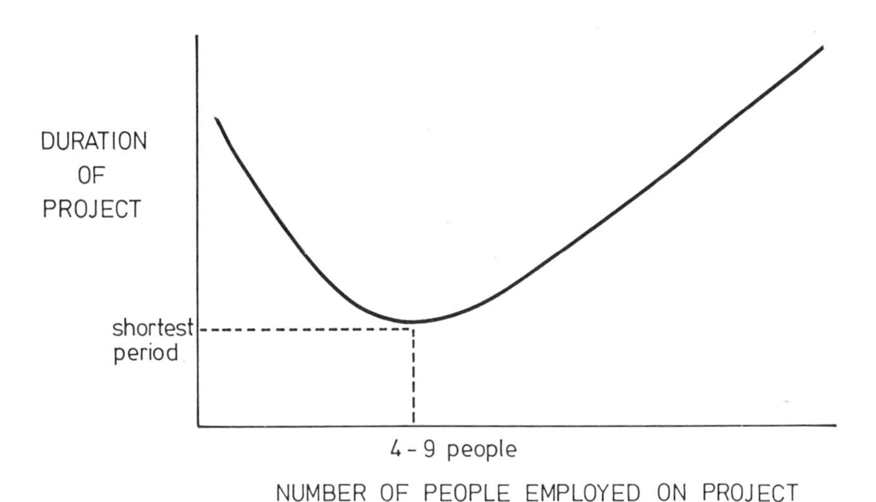

Figure 5: *The Myth of Man Years*

increases so productivity will increase, although not linearly. As more people become involved so the inherent problems of group working become manifest. Communication between members becomes more difficult and time consuming. Productivity declines, see Figure 5.

There is an optimum number of people who can work together. This number will vary according to the task, the personality of the members and the quality of the leadership. Of course, this does not preclude dividing the overall task into smaller tasks, as mentioned earlier, and giving each subtask to a group of people, thus speeding the development process. You should remember that each group will have its problems and the total number of groups you can handle is similar to the total number of individuals. Each group is an 'individual'. The more groups you have, the more problems you will encounter.

NET PRESENT VALUE

Which would you rather have: £1000 now or £2000 in five years time? Assuming that you do not reject the offer out of hand, your decision will be influenced by two factors. Firstly, you will consider how desperate you are for cash. It is not unheard of for individuals and even organisations to be short of cash. In these circumstances you may opt for the cash now. If you have no immediate cash problems you will consider the second factor, what will the £2000 be worth in five years compared with the £1000? If inflation is high then the £2000 may only be worth £1000 in real terms. You should also take into account the interest that would accrue if you took the £1000 and invested the money in a bank. Adding these together, it is preferable to take the £1000 despite the fact that it is obviously half of the £2000 on offer.

This example illustrates the notion of net present value. If we are considering the development of an expert system, we have to consider the immediate expenditure against rewards that will not accrue for what may be several years. If we are suffering a cash flow problem, we will reject any suggestion of investing in an expert system. If we have money available, we have to consider which is the best use of that money. Putting the money into a bank may produce higher rewards than building an expert system that will produce no results for a long time. On the other hand, we could calculate that the benefits will far outweigh the costs. The more rigorous we are in considering both costs and benefits, the more likely we are to choose expert system applications that are successful.

SUMMARY

Whilst we may feel that an expert system might be a good idea, such a system is not always viable. This chapter considered how to choose areas that would be suitable for creating a knowledge base, using the following criteria: size, complexity, current formulation, regularity of use and the nature of the information. It continued with a review of cost/benefit analysis, looking particularly at the problems of estimation of time and costs in software projects. This chapter concluded with an explanation of net present value and its relevance to cost/benefit analysis. Of course, not all costs and benefits can be translated into cash terms. Whilst we can itemise most costs and benefits, in the end implementing an expert system will be a strategic rather than a financial decision. However, we should be aware of the financial implications, both positive and negative, as far as we are able.

4
Building a System

INTRODUCTION

In Chapter three we considered how to select suitable areas for developing an expert system. This chapter continues with a look at some of the important things to consider when developing a system and some of the tasks and roles involved in the process comparing these with the traditional approach to developing computer-based systems.

THE SYSTEMS LIFE CYCLE

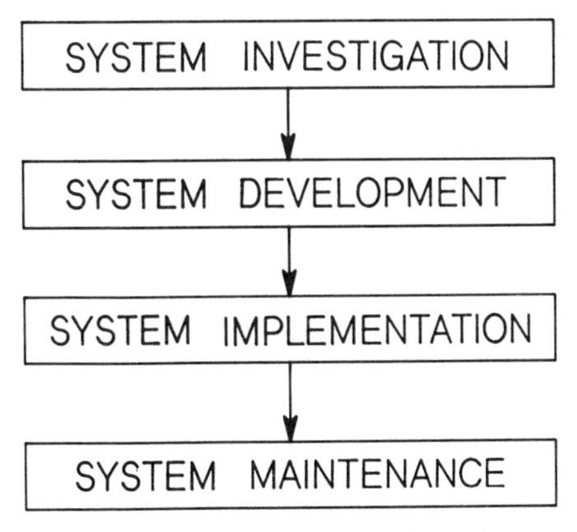

Figure 6: *The Systems Life Cycle*

In the past, computer-based systems have been developed following the stages of the systems life cycle, see Figure 6. The initial stage is the system investigation. A manager may feel that they have a problem which could be resolved using a computer. Let us assume that the manager is responsible for invoicing customers. The manager must raise invoices, send them to customers, keep track of those that have been paid and chase those that have yet to be paid. There is scope for a computer system here. The manager would contact the data processing or information systems department depending on the label being used. Some time later, the length of time will vary from one organisation to another, a specialist from the data processing department will call on the manager to discuss the problem. The specialist will probably be a systems analyst. Following discussion the analyst will produce a statement of user requirements. A feasibility study with a cost/benefit analysis will determine if the system is viable. If the system is viable the next stage will start.

The system development starts with a complete analysis of the problem, which will involve full discussion between the data processing specialist and the manager. Once the discussions are complete the project is in the hands of the data processing department. During this stage both the software and hardware will be specified and ordered. Any software not already available will be commissioned by the analyst to be written by inhouse programmers or a software house. During the development the various parts of the system will be tested.

Once the system has been developed the project can move into the system implementation phase. There are several different methods for implementing systems. Firstly, one can use a pilot scheme whereby the system is implemented in one part of the organisation or one part of the system is implemented to iron out the problems. The pilot could involve a smaller, more basic, version of the final system, a prototype which is cheaper and easier to develop and which could be changed prior to final implementation. Another method of implementation is a parallel run, where the old manual system and the new computer system run side by side for a limited period. This is particularly helpful for checking that the new system behaves itself, for example, computer produced invoices can be compared with manually produced invoices, to establish that the system is doing what it should. Implementation can be phased, that is introduced to different parts of the organisation at different times, for example, producing computer invoices for one factory and then another and so on. This is a lengthy procedure but it can be a useful approach because it enables local problems to be identified. Sometimes it is not possible to have the advantages of parallel or phased implementation. The system may be implemented using the bigbang approach, at 8.59 a.m. it is the old system and at 9.00 a.m. it is the new system. Changing from driving on the right to the left would require such an approach. The big bang changes of the London Stock Market happened almost in this way although there was some scope for testing the system before it went live. The big bang approach is fraught with problems. Generally it is possible to use a gentler method of implemetation. Of course, the methods described above can be combined, with a pilot leading to a phased implemetation or a prototype leading to a parallel run.

Once the system is implemented the next stage is system maintenance. This will involve maintenance of both hardware and software, correcting any errors that arise, upgrading the system where necessary and handling future problems. By this stage the computer specialist will have handed the problem and, hopefully, the solution back to the manager although the data processing department will retain an interest in maintaining the hardware and software.

The systems life cycle has a remarkable neatness rarely seen in practice. The development process is not simple and straightforward because neither users nor analysts have a clear idea of their requirements at the outset. Rather than a progression through the four stages, systems development is a reiterative process. Often changes to requirements are made during the programming stage because of limitations in hardware, software, outputs or inputs. Nonetheless some principles hold good. The system development starts with a germ of an idea. This is then handed over to computer specialists who develop the solution which may or may not actually match the users requirements.

There are some similarities between developing traditional systems and expert systems. They both start with an idea that there is a problem that a computer could solve. This should be followed by a clear definition of the problem, the user requirements and a cost/benefit analysis. Once set up the expert system will have to be maintained in the same way that a traditional system has to be. It is the development and implementation stages that are different. Developing expert systems requires the close involvement of the expert, or experts, whose knowledge is being encapsulated in the knowledge base. This is unlike a traditional system which can be developed by analysts and programmers in isolation from the problem. Furthermore, an expert system is trying to store and access knowledge not handle data. Knowledge bases are built whereas computer programs are written. The implementation of expert system applications can be gradual, perhaps even phased. We can use other traditional methods, such as prototyping, to develop expert systems. Nonetheless, we need to rethink how expert system applications are developed. The roles and tasks involved in developing such applications are not identical to those in developing traditional systems. The systems analyst together with a group of programmers taking over the problem from a manager have been replaced by an expert, a knowledge engineer and a knowledge base administrator working side by side.

PEOPLE INVOLVED IN DEVELOPING AN EXPERT SYSTEM

The advertising literature suggests that the development of an expert system is something that is done single handed. The expert sits down

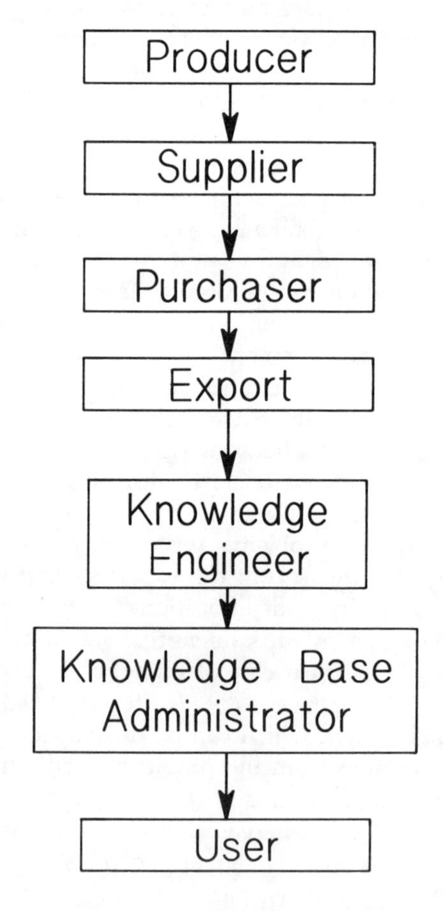

Figure 7: *The Development Chain*

at his computer, writes a set of rules covering the knowledge, tidies it up and then hands over the resulting product to any user that wants to use it. Whilst it could happen like this, it is more likely that a group of people are involved. Perhaps as expert systems develop and improve an expert could create their own application. Meanwhile, someone intending to develop a system should be aware of the various people that are involved.

THE PRODUCER OF THE SHELL

There is a long chain of people involved in the development of expert system applications. The first link in this chain is the producer of the expert system shell that will be used. There is nothing remarkable about such producers. They range from large corporations, who have produced a shell for their own use and are willing to sell it publicly, to individual researchers who have small expert systems that they are offering to the public. There is a listing of producers in Chapter 12, included are names you may recognise: Carnegie, Ferranti, ICL, Texas Instruments, etc., as well as companies specialising in Artificial Intelligence: Artificial Intelligence Ltd, Intelligence Products, Intelligent Terminals Ltd, etc. One small but significant difference between expert systems and most other software packages is the producer of the software is also the supplier. At the moment anybody wishing to purchase an expert system shell will go directly to the producer rather than buying a shell from an independent dealer. This direct buying is reflected in the level of advertising by the producers themselves to attract customers. In the future as expert systems become established it is likely that they will be sold by dealers from the same shelf as spreadsheets, text processors and databases.

THE PURCHASER

It is interesting to speculate who buys experts system shells. We know that most of the top one thousand companies have bought an expert system shell because the suppliers tell us this is so. But who bought them, by which I mean who signed the purchasing order? Some large organisations, such as those searching for oil, have developed their own systems whilst at the other end of the scale the one-man business has yet to implement any new technology. Perhaps it is the medium to large organisations that are buying expert systems, but the question still remains who is it within the organisation actually responsible for paying for a shell from their budget. I suspect it is not 'experts' or managers buying shells, rather it is individuals within data processing departments who are buying shells 'to try them out'. If you are not working in a data processing department, and, perhaps, even if you do, it is worth asking if somebody has already bought an expert system shell and has started to use it. The important point here is that purchasers are not experts or users. It is a long path from the supplier through the purchaser to the expert and, eventually, the user.

THE EXPERT

A popular misconception is that there is an expert who holds all the knowledge about to be embodied within an expert system. More likely the knowledge is held by several people. Alternatively, the knowledge is not held by an expert at all but is contained within the documentation of the organisation or body. It would be possible to draw up an expert system based on the Offices, Shops and Railway Premises Act, or, indeed, any other piece of legislation. Whilst a legal beagle somewhere in the world may know the contents of the act inside out it is not necessary to even talk to them if the act itself is available. Indeed the original holder of the knowledge may be dead and buried if the Act was passed several decades ago. Thus the knowledge can be contained in a head, several heads, in the written word, and eventually in a computer's memory, and the computer will create an expert system using its own knowledge. A combination using an expert's knowledge and the written word is a good source for a knowledge base giving the official information and also a practitioner's view of the world.

THE KNOWLEDGE BASE ENGINEER

A knowledge base engineer (KBE) is a person with intimate knowledge of an expert system shell, experience in creating applications and the ability to extract knowledge from an expert or experts. How to extract knowledge is discussed in more detail below. It is the role of the knowledge base engineer to extract it. Clearly there are advantages to using a KBE who may be an individual in your organisation, a person from the company who sold you the shell or an independent consultant. An 'expert' who has spent a lifetime researching this knowledge base is not likely to be adept in developing expert systems, unless, of course, that was the lifetime's work. Until expert systems have become fully interactive and user friendly a third party is an invaluable asset, which may be costly but will save hours and hours of fruitless work and will increase the chances of success.

THE KNOWLEDGE BASE ADMINISTRATOR

Just as setting up an expert system is a complex activity, maintaining a system so that it remains accurate, up-to-date and useful is also a specialised activity and is the role of the knowledge base administrator (KBA). You may feel an administator is a little excessive for a small expert system, but when your systems grow to be several hundred rules then someone needs to understand how it is constructed, what the underlying assumptions were and how best to interrogate the knowledge. The expert, knowledge base engineer and knowledge base administrator may be one and the same person if the system is small and local. However, as the system grows and it is dissipated with more and more remote users the roles become more easily identifiable and thus separable.

THE USER

It is argued, especially by sellers of expert system shells, that expert system applications are friendly and helpful to the user. This is only true if the shell has the facility to be helpful and friendly and the person creating the knowledge base is aware of the end user of the system and creates the system accordingly. An expert system, like any other computer system, is only as friendly as the developer makes it. Remember the user! If possible involve the user in the development process, taking note of their comments and suggestions. Paradoxically, the better and more helpful the system, the more it will teach the user. Consequently, it will be used less and less by the user as the user gets to know it more and more, rather like the instructions with a compact disk player or video recorder. The more you use the equipment the less you need the instructions.

BUILDING A KNOWLEDGE BASE

There are several stages in building a knowledge base. The first is to identify the area of expertise that you wish to embody in the knowledge base using the criteria given above. It is then necessary to identify who will create the knowledge base and determine what the sources of knowledge will be, enlisting the aid of the relevant experts.

If you do not have an expert system shell then you will need to choose and purchase one from the wide range available. It will then be possible to encapsulate the knowledge in rules. Once the rules are created, the help can be added and the system can be tested to ensure it works properly. Like the traditional systems life cycle mentioned earlier, this is a simplistic view of the world. The development of a knowledge base will be a reiterative process with rules being redefined and rewritten as the knowledge base grows. This development process assumes that you have an expert system shell rather than building a complete expert system from scratch. Available shells are considered in Chapter nine.

As stated in Chapter three, it is impossible to give accurate initial forecasts of the time required to build a system. However, if you are building a reasonably large system, it will take 6–24 months to build a prototype. Having completed a prototype it may take ten times that length of time for a full implementation to be completed. An alternative way of determining the length of the project is to estimate the number of rules required for the system and allocate one day per rule. Thus a small system of thirty rules will take one month, a larger system using one hundred rules will take three months, and a big system with a thousand rules will take almost three years. This may seem daunting but compares favourably with other system's development times, such as large databases.

CREATING A SET OF RULES

All rule-based expert system shells will have a facility for entering rules into a knowledge base. However, this facility may vary from a simple, unhelpful, unfriendly text editor to a sophisticated knowledge base editor. The more expensive the shell, the more sophisticated the editor is likely to be. The more powerful have a range of inbuilt devices to make life easier, such as, automatic numbering and dating of rules, automatic checking of consistency and automatic entry of rules into a rule library.

Any expert system application will be structured according to the expert system shell that is used. In other words the knowledge base must be created to suit the shell. Some will handle only text, some will handle text and numbers and some will handle uncertainty, more of which later. Meanwhile, remember you do not have absolute control over the structure of the knowledge base, it must fit the model. Nonetheless, you do have control over the knowledge and you should consider how the knowledge is structured. If possible partition the knowledge into meaningful subsections. This enables the knowledge base engineer to work on a bit at a time. Also, it means that subsequent interrogation will be faster because related items are stored together. It will make testing easier because each subsection can be tested and verified independently. Finally, it will make subsequent maintenance easier because a structured knowledge base with identifiable subsections will be more self-evident. Having emphasised the constraints on rules, how can we identify what the rules are? Establishing rules can be done in three ways or a combination of these three.

Firstly, rules can be based on past experience. In the past things have happened, rules have been adhered to in practice even if they are not written down. Creating the rule base is a matter of remembering the rules, or better still the knowledge base engineer talking to the expert and building a picture of the knowledge and then creating it as a set of rules. The KBE will probably use a tape recorder to create a permanent record of the conversation so that the discussion about the knowledge is not hampered by the need to create rules to fit the model. Turning the knowledge into rules can be done subsequently. A conversation would be 'what happened if the ...' with the response 'well I always found that ...'.

Secondly, rules can be based on the present. An expert can sit down and analyse their current behaviour. This is particularly useful when attempting to embody skills in an expert system. What does an engineer do when fixing your television set? Why not watch the engineer at work, asking questions about what he is doing and why, perhaps videotaping the whole procedure so that the knowledge base engineer can go back and check detail and then formulate the rules? The conversation would be 'why are you doing that...' and the response 'I always test this first so that I know it is not the widget, then I can go on and test the ...'.

Thirdly, rules can be based on future possible events. This is useful for two reasons. Making enquiries about the past or even the present may not elicit all possibilities. Alternatively, we may not have had examples of all occurrences or may not want them, for example, we do not want to experience breakdown of production, leakage of waste, an epidemic, a large disaster, etc. Nonetheless, we would want to encapsulate as much knowledge as we have in the knowledge base, even if it is hypothetical. A conversation would be 'what would you do if ...' with the response 'we are likely to do x, y and z'. These three approaches are known as retrospective, episodic and propositional.

There are inherent difficulties in creating knowledge bases using experts' knowledge. There is a mismatch between the way an expert stores knowledge and the way a knowledge base stores knowledge which makes getting the knowledge into the base the hardest part of developing a system. There are several solutions available to this problem, known as the 'engineering bottleneck'. Currently, the solution is to use a knowledge base engineer who is practised in the art of knowledge acquistion thus giving the benefit of past experience. An alternative is to avoid creating rules altogether and use a rule-inducing shell, described in Chapter ten. In the future the solution will be an automated knowledge acquisition system that interrogates experts, reads text books and formulates rules.

BLACKBOARDING

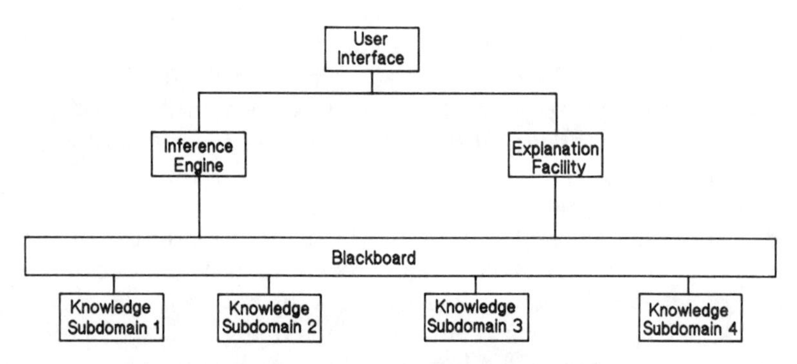

Figure 8: *A Blackboard Structure*

One further problem of knowledge acquisition is that the knowledge that we want to encapsulate within a knowledge base is not held in one source. It is possible that the knowledge is held by several experts, each of whom have a particular area of expertise which, when brought together, will give a useful expert system application. The problem remains of how to combine the seperate knowledge domains. One approach, first attempted in the mid 1970s and still being researched, is 'blackboarding'. Imagine that the experts write on a blackboard everything they know pertaining to a problem. The inference engine can link the knowledge together selecting those parts that are relevant. However, such a blackboard could be very large. It may be better to cluster each expert's knowledge together on subdomains and then call up the knowledge when necessary. To keep track of what is where, and in which subdomain, is the responsibility of the blackboard, see Figure 8. This blackboard is a large and complex database. To handle this complexity the computer must be powerful and capable of parallel processing, that is, performing several tasks at the same time. There are a limited number of such machines available. As the next group of computers are developed, the so-called fifth generation, parallel processing will become more widely available and blackboarding may be a feature of all expert systems large or small.

THE NOTION OF PROBABILITY

So far we have considered rules as simple condition–action pairs:

if it is raining
then I will take an umbrella

Such pairs assume that the causality, that is, the link between them, is always going to happen. In other words, if it is raining I will always take an umbrella. However, the world is not so absolute. We are not always sure that the outcome is always going to happen, for example:

if he has spots
then he has measles

is not a very convincing rule because we know spots can be caused by other things such as acne, chicken pox or even painting a ceiling. So within our expert system we need a way of handling this uncertainty. It may be that we can add rules together so that eventually we can be absolutely certain or almost certain, for example, if a person is painting his ceiling, the spots are the same colour as the paint and there are no other symptoms we may assume with reasonable certainty that the person has paint spots and not measles. However, we can only arrive at this certainty after considering uncertainty so how can this be incorporated in a system? The simplest approach is to include uncertainty within the rule such as

if he has spots
then it is likely he has measles

This is not a problem for the shell because we are simply extending the action clause. As long as the condition–action pair is in the form if... then...

we can include any qualifiers that we think are helpful. These can be simply likely or unlikely or on a scale of certainty from absolutely certain through highly likely, likely etc., to absolutely uncertain. Combining uncertainties can give certainties. Consider the following rules:

if the sky is grey and the barometer is falling
then it is likely to rain

if it is likely to rain
then I will carry an umbrella

Even though we are not certain about the weather, if we tell the system it is grey and the barometer is falling it will tell us to carry an umbrella, thus creating certainty from uncertainty. However, if we are to combine several rules that include uncertainty we can use a different approach.

Whilst some shells allow the development of rules as a series of statements with uncertainty as part of the text, other shells allow you to allocate a level of certainty when each rule is entered. (Some shells give you the option of both.) This level of certainty is entered as a probability. So what is probability? It is a scale from 0 to 1 depending upon your confidence that something will happen. We know that I will never fly and this we can assign a probability of 0. On the other hand we know that it will rain in Manchester and this we assign 1. Of course there are various levels of probability in between. If you spin a coin what is the probability it will come down heads? Well we know it can only be heads or tails (unless there is some dishonesty). We say there is a fifty/fifty chance of heads. This means that half the time it will be heads and half the time it will be tails. The probability of heads is 0.5 or 1/2. Similarly, the probability of tails is 0.5 or 1/2. You may have noticed that 0.5 plus 0.5 = 1, which is absolute certainty. This is reasonable since we can be absolutely certain the coin will be heads or tails. There are no other possibilities. Generally the following applies:

$$\text{probability of event occurring} = \frac{\text{number of ways event can occur}}{\text{number of alternatives}}$$

To extend the discussion a little, what is the probability that we will select a heart from a pack of cards? We know a pack contains 13 hearts and there are 52 cards in total. We can evaluate that there is a probabilty of 13/52 or 1/4 or 0.25 that we will draw a heart. Similarly, there is a probability of 0.25 that we will draw a diamond, spade or club. Again all four probabilities must equal 1, that is 0.25 + 0.25 + 0.25 + 0.25.

Probabilities can be added, so the probability of selecting a red card is the probability of selecting a heart and a diamond, that is, 0.25 + 0.25 = 0.5. Similarly, probabilities can be multiplied, where options are related but not mutually exclusive. As an example, we know the probability of getting a head is 0.5. If we toss two coins what is the probability of two heads? Well it is 0.5 * 0.5 = 0.25 or 1 in 4. This makes sense if we consider the options that can happen, which are:

tail/tail
tail/head
head/tail
head/head

Of the four possible outcomes only one is head/head giving the probability of 0.25, also known as 1 in 4 or 25%.

When creating a set of rules each is given a probability (p) and these are combined by being either added or multiplied, according to the context, so that the eventual outcome is given with an associated probability. Complex sets of probability are handled by a technique using something called Bayes' Theorem. Discussing the theorem in detail is beyond the scope of this book. Suffice it to say that a collection of rules each with an associated probability can be combined to give an outcome with a probability, for example:

if the patient has spots
    then the patient has measles p = 0.45

if the patient has a temperature
    then the patient has measles p = 0.20

if the patient has a sore throat
    then the patient has measles p = 0.35

if all three statements are true the outcome could be:

the patient has measles with p = 0.78

Such a probability may compare favourably with a doctor's degree of certainty in diagnosis.

Just as uncertainty can be included in rules, it can also be included in responses. Thus if the system asks 'Does the patient have a rash?' the response can be yes or no, a simple text response or a number giving the degree of certainty of the user, for example 0.5 to show the user is uncertain one way or the other. Whilst it appears more 'scientific' to quantify all rules and responses this is not necessarily the case. Rather it may be better to simplify the system as much as possible. A system that handles faults in a system does not want uncertainty. Either the boiler is going to blow up or it isn't. To handle such contingencies it is easier to use simplified categories such as yes or no. Why confuse the system with too much data? Either the water pressure, say, is getting higher (=+), staying the same (=0) or decreasing (=-). In this way uncertainty and ambiguity are reduced.

Finally, we can say with some certainty that current versions of expert systems are limited in the way they deal with uncertainty. As they improve they will be able to cope better with human uncertainty. There is a great deal of research focused in this area known as 'fuzzy logic', which attempts to cope with the world and its imperfections.

CREATING A HELP SYSTEM

Having created a set of rules with or without associated probabilities, the person constructing the system, albeit the expert himself or a knowledge base engineer, will need to consider the help given by the system. One obvious benefit of an expert system compared with traditional computer programs is their interactiveness and associated help facilities. However, as stated above, help must be built in at the construction stage. It will not materialise.

The simplest level of help, and that most commonly found in expert systems, is a restatement of the rule. A user may be asked the question:

```
Does the person have spots?
Respond Yes/No/Don't know/Why Y,N,D or W
```

If a user asks why, they will be told:

```
RULE 87: if the patient has spots
         then the patient has measles p = 0.45
```

This may be rewritten to say:

> I am trying to establish if the patient has spots because this will give a 45% certain prediction that he has measles.

Whilst it may be helpful to know which rule is being used by the system there could be more informative help available, which is entered at the time the rule itself is entered. Who entered the rule? Was the rule entered at the inception of the system or was it added later? Why is the rule supposed to work? What does it add to the overall system? Other information can be built up during the working life of the system. Has it been invoked in the past? How well has it worked in the past? All of these questions actually help the user to understand the role of the question in the system and should help the user in framing their answer to the initial enquiry 'Does the person have spots?' Linked to the help can be a screen of supporting material such as text and graphics known as a frame. Currently being developed are expert systems that link to advanced laser video disks. Asking why, in the future, could mean not only an explanation of the question, but also some explanatory text and some moving colour pictures of spots with which you can make comparisons.

Also under the help heading we need to consider user intervention. It is likely that the user will become very familiar with the system and want to truncate or bypass some parts of it. Why should the user go through the section on measles when he knows the patient cannot possibly have measles? To cope with this the shell should have the ability to listen. In other words, because the knowledge is partitioned into related areas it is possible for the user to tell the system certain items which will exclude sections and speed up the interrogative process.

Finally, a system needs to handle people who disagree with it. What happens if the user goes through the interrogation but disagrees with the conclusion because he has evidence not considered by the expert system? Can the system cope with apparent ambiguity, extend its rule base to include the added knowledge or retain ambiguity within the rules? Most current implementations of expert systems on personal computers do not have the robustness to handle such delicate problems during interrogation, but the knowledge base can be extended at a later date. During interrogation rules are rules and have to be obeyed.

Generally, the system should be as helpful as possible. Some of the help is inherent in the expert system shell but some is added in the particular application. To maximise help, as much thought as possible should be given to the user. A lot of attention is at last being given to users and this should be reflected in expert systems. The software world is discovering that it is possible to make life easier by using different colours on the screen, segmenting the screen into different parts (windows) or using an electronic pointer (mouse) rather than trying to type in endlessly. All these benefits aid the user and improve the quality of the system. There appear to be cultural differences in the level of help provided. The Americans and Japanese are much keener on colour and graphics than their austere European contemporaries.

TESTING A SYSTEM

Having developed a system the final requirement is to test it as far as possible before it is used. A small knowledge base may be almost perfect but as size increases so problems are likely to arise. However, since the rules are input by the relevant expert, or alternatively by a knowledge base engineer based on discussions with and verified by the expert or experts, there should be no problem with the final application. Nonetheless as systems grow in size and complexity there may be inherent problems in the knowledge base. There are four areas of concern:

VALIDITY

The first question to ask is about the validity of the system. Does the system actually help solve the problems or give guidance in the areas stated in the original idea? It is all too easy to have an idea for a system which eventually is unsuccessful because the wrong knowledge is gathered in the knowledge base. If the system is not entirely successful then the knowledge base engineer should go back to the criteria for selecting projects listed above and determine why it failed. Was it too trivial, too large or was the knowledge just not available?

SCOPE

The next question to ask is about the scope of the system. Does the knowledge base cover all the area required and all contingencies that may arise? What happens if the user starts to stray from the coverage of the system? For example, the application may be medical and cover a range of illnesses but obviously cannot cover all of them. If the symptoms presented by the patient and typed in by the doctor/user are outside the scope of the system will it inform the user of this important fact or will it respond there is no disease? Any system must be aware of its own boundaries and should inform the user when these boundaries or limits have been reached by the user. This definition of boundaries is known as 'scoping'.

RELIABILITY

If the system gives answers or outcomes which are relevant and useful, are they reliable? If the user pursues the same responses twice will the outcome be the same? If the user follows two paths through the system but gives the same answer will the outcome be the same? To test reliability requires the knowledge base engineer to enter answers during interrogation that test the limits of the system, to establish if and where the system will fail.

One particular question to ask is how the expert system copes with the unexpected. It may be that you have a perfectly adequate application that helps you decide when to buy and sell stocks and shares. The decisions will be triggered by world events such as changes in interest rates, overseas investment, etc. But what happens if the world changes in a new and strange way, for example, the often cited Wall Street Crash? It is likely that your system will not only be confused by the external disaster but will also contribute to the disaster by selling all your shares. Your expert system application knows that when prices start to fall it should sell, thus contributing to the crash. Unfortunately, not all contingencies can be foreseen and allowed for within an expert system. There could be circumstances where a complete reversal of the rules are necessary. The application should inform you when it meets completely unexpected circumstances.

LEGALITY

As computers in general, and artificial intelligence in particular, become more widespread, the question of responsibility becomes increasingly important. This is certainly true for expert systems. Suppose a system is used as an aid to diagnose in a hospital and the system suggests a course of treatment that proves injurious. There are few systems available now upon which one would have total reliance. However, the time is not far off when it will be so, given all the research and effort in this area. So who is liable? The doctor who used the system is an obvious choice. But what of the expert who drew up the rules or the knowledge base engineer who put these rules into a system? Finally what about the system itself? Can a computer system or an application running on that system be considered liable. Indeed, is the supplier of the expert system shell also liable?

For the moment systems are small and augment human knowledge and experience. The responsibility for the diagnosis and treatment rests with the doctor. Similarly, the responsibility for the car repair rests with the mechanic not the fault finding expert system. However, expert systems are designed to replace experts and eventually we may have interactive diagnostic systems for ourselves and our car. Where is the human minding the system? Who is responsible for it then? The need for some legislation is self evident and the first test case of a patient suing an expert system should give impetus to the much needed discussion. As systems become more complex, less of the rules and assumptions will be known to the user. Coupled with increasing dependency the user becomes more and more vulnerable. Using a system becomes more of a gamble. A system is not a legal entity (yet) and therefore cannot be sued but one day who knows?

DIFFICULTIES IN BUILDING AN EXPERT SYSTEM

Building an expert system, like developing any software application, is fraught with possible disaster. It is worthwhile to reiterate the potential areas of trouble.

THE KNOWLEDGE DOMAIN

An error in choosing the wrong domain may not become apparent until you are well into the development process. To avoid this pitfall use the criteria in Chapter three to identify a suitable area and start with a prototype version. If the project does falter, accept defeat and if you are sure the project will not succeed then abandon it. It is better to divert attention to a new project than keep going with a lame duck.

EXPERT SYSTEM SHELLS

Shells are comparatively new with the oldest still less than ten years old and most one or two years old. Choose a reputable shell and devote the necessary time and effort to ensure that those involved in a project can use it. Generate realistic targets for completion dates. The optimism of suppliers may lead to unrealistic targets which in turn may lead to frustration.

PEOPLE

It is possible that top management have no commitment to expert systems. Furthermore, those involved in developing systems may be under resourced with too few staff, too little time and not enough skills. For any project to succeed the commitment must be there from the top down. Expert system applications are not things that can be developed by people in their spare time. There should be corporate support and commitment. Time and effort must be devoted to training all those involved in the application, from developers to users.

THE EXPERTS

The experts, whose knowledge is being embodied in the knowledge base, should be available and accessible. Maintaining the enthusiasm of the expert or experts is a difficult task. Ensure that they are fully committed at the outset of the project and maintain their interest by keeping them involved, allowing them to see the knowledge base being developed.

KNOWLEDGE ACQUISITION

Knowledge acquisition, the bottleneck of developing applications, is not a clearly defined science. At best it is an art practised by the few. Ensure that sufficient resources are available to reduce any pressure on those involved. If possible, use a knowledge engineer or a consultant from the company who supplied the shell to help the development process. Again the use of a prototype will identify particular problem areas.

TESTING

The science of testing like the science of acquisition is almost nonexistent. Test the knowledge base as it is built, maintain a reasonable structure so that the various parts of the knowledge domain can be tested. Trace through the knowledge base to check rules and use extreme cases to test how your application will cope.

An expert system shell is deliberately constructed so that the inferences are carried out by the shell. The user may know the rules and the expert may be familiar with the knowledge base but there is an intervening process not open to either. Indeed, suppliers are loath to give information about how their products actually work because of the fear of other software manufacturers pirating the ideas. Perhaps suppliers should be more open about the way their shells actually work.

TIME

Despite good estimations of the times required to finish a development and good project management to ensure that such times are adhered to during the development, most projects run over time. Take your original estimate of the time required, double it and add ten months or years depending on the timescale you are using. This does not preclude the necessity of either time estimates or good project management, but be aware that projects can, and do, run late and do not allow such lateness to build up further frustration and tension.

SUMMARY

This chapter, having looked at the traditional approach to systems development, went on to discuss developing expert system applications. Firstly, it considered the people involved in developing a system. The expert, knowledge base engineer, knowledge base administrator and user may not be separate people but the roles are clearly identifiable and all have a part to play. Then it looked at the stages in building a knowledge base starting with rules and considering help facilities within the system. Several expert system shell packages use the probability of events occuring as a way of creating rules. Consequently, the notion of probability was discussed in some detail. Next, this chapter considered the testing of a knowledge base looking at validity, scope, reliabilty and some of the legal implications. Finally it reviewed some of the difficulties that can be encountered when developing an expert system application.

5

Maintaining and Updating an Expert System

INTRODUCTION

Any expert system developed will not remain static. As the world changes and our knowledge changes so the knowledge base must change. Of course, this is made easier using an expert system shell because the inference engine is not part of the knowledge base. In other words we can add, change or delete rules in the knowledge base without worrying about how the changes will affect the overall system. The inference engine will take any changes or modifications into account during interrogation. This chapter will consider why such changes may be necessary, how such changes can be made and how the total system will be affected. Finally, it will consider the necessary steps to be taken to ensure the security of an expert system.

THE NEED FOR UPDATES

In Chapter one we observed that an expert system is a static view of the world. The rules embodied in a system reflect a unitary view of a knowledge area or domain. The rules will reflect the knowledge of possibly one expert, using one life time's experience and created at a point in time. It requires little imagination to realise that any of these things may change. A short tale to remind ourselves that things are not constant.

One day the court jester upset the king who ordered him to be killed. The jester asked the king to spare his life for one year and he would teach his horse to fly. If at the end of the year the horse could not fly the jester would be executed. The king agreed but the jester's friend thought that he was mad, simply delaying the inevitable and having to spend a gloomy year under sentence of death. The jester pointed out that a lot could happen in a year. The king could change his mind, the king might die, the jester himself might die anyway, the horse might die and, who knows, he might even teach the horse to fly.

So it is with an expert system. Having created the system as the perfect, never changing, right for ever system, someone will want to change it. Impetus for change can originate from several sources:

EXPERT

In Chapter one a limitation of expert systems was shown to be their inability to reflect more than one point in time. However, an expert may want to change the rules because of advances in knowledge or perhaps even changes in knowledge. As experience and understanding grows, so the knowledge base must cope with these changes.

KNOWLEDGE BASE ENGINEER

It is the knowledge base engineer who bridges the gap between the expert who may know nothing of computer systems and the expert system itself. The engineer may wish to change the base because of perceived inadequacies in the system. Such changes would include rewriting the rules to make navigation through the rules easier and quicker, combining the knowledge base with a related knowledge base, extending the application of the system or combining the expert system with existing decision support software.

KNOWLEDGE BASE ADMINISTRATOR

As the system is disseminated to users, which is what it is intended for, it is possible that generic problems may arise which affect the whole user base. The knowledge base administrator will have overall responsibility for the system. It may require changes and modifications to redefine the limits or scope of the knowledge domain. The supplier of the expert system shell may provide an improved version of the shell which the administrator will want to use. This may not affect the actual rules but it will affect the running of the system. A new version may be faster, more helpful, have a colour screen or be more interactive. Since expert systems are comparatively new, they are likely to be more prone to upgrades and improvements than more established software packages. Indeed, most shells available, which are listed in Chapter nine, are not the original version of the package but are version two or the 'Plus' version with refinements.

USER

Each user will become an expert, if not in the subject itself then at least as a user of the system about the subject. As knowledge and confidence grows so the user may want more control over the system, with the ability to modify rules that do not work in a particular context, to disregard parts of the system that are irrelevant and generally to tailor the application to suit their own needs. Users may also want to intervene during an interrogative session and change rules that they disagree with. All contingencies, including user interventions, must be handled successfully by the system.

However, allowing the user to update the system can lead to serious problems. Some systems are specifically created to control a process, such as manufacturing. In these examples the user, that is, the manufacturing process, should not influence the expert system. Other systems are designed to give advice not control. Users may be allowed to accept or reject advice without affecting the system. On the other hand they may be allowed to intervene in the system and change the system to suit their requirements. As they are allowed more access to the system and make more changes, so the system will look less like the original. If there are several users all modifying the system, eventually there will be a range of systems all with the same name but completely different. The alternative is to have no user intervention at all, but this denies the ability of the user to learn and improve the knowledge base. It is better to allow for changes but control these changes via the knowledge base administrator through a 'users group'. If a change is valid for one user, then it ought to be valid for others and should be incorporated in all copies of the system.

CHANGING THE RULES

As can be seen, changes to the knowledge base can be instigated from a variety of people. These changes will require modifications to the rules. This is simple and straightforward if the knowledge base is small, say 50 or even 100 rules. It becomes increasingly more difficult as the knowledge base grows. As a system reaches full size, say 1000 rules, so the task of updating the knowledge base becomes very difficult indeed. There are two distinct problems. The first is finding the rule which requires modification and the second is knowing the effect that change will have on the total system. Fortunately, the inference engine will handle any changes made and will invoke rules whenever they are necessary. Therefore a change to a rule which alters the contents of the rule base will be handled by the inference engine. As an example, let us suppose that the system is used for fault finding and suggesting remedies. It may be company policy that serious breakdowns require the call out of a senior engineer thus:

If breakdown is serious
  Then call out senior engineer

However, with better training (using expert systems of course) and an improvement in breakdown repairs (again using an expert system) the engineers may be able to cope with all breakdowns without recourse to senior engineers. Following a change in company policy, the rule will be:

If breakdown is serious
  Then call out engineer

This changed rule will invoke a series of questions about who is the call out engineer, what he or she should do, etc. Similarly, the expert system will go on and give advice about solving the problem and remedying the breakdown. The inference engine will automatically search for these questions given the new rule. Thus changing one rule could substantially alter the way the system works without having to go through all questions.

However, there will be occasions when you may want to change not one rule but sets of rules relating to one area. How do you find these rules in the midst of a thousand others? Firstly, your knowledge base should be divided or partitioned into meaningful parts so that related rules are close together as much as possible. Thus, changing a rule or even inserting a new rule is a more local process. This has a useful but limited contribution since inevitably there will be cross partition links between rules, otherwise the various parts of the knowledge base will not interrelate at all and you will be left with a collection of smaller unrelated knowledge bases. Clearly it is better if you have some way of keeping track of rules, and this is available with some expert system shells in the form of a rule dictionary.

Any rule will consist of three essential parts. For example:

Rule 658

a condition—if it is raining

and

an action—then I will take an umbrella

Each rule will have a condition, an action and an identification number. Additionally, rules will have associated help which could be simply a restatement of the rule, which is tautological: you will take an umbrella because it is raining; or a more complex explanation such as those suggested in Chapter three: you do not like getting wet and will carry an umbrella to keep yourself dry, I know you do not like getting wet because you answered no when asked about rule 345, etc. Some packages will also have pages of text or frames to help the user. If the system is specifically constructed for use as a computer-based teaching package then frames are central to the system. Each frame may contain text, pictures or both.

However, a rule may have one further addition, a dictionary entry or entries which will be entered by the person developing the system. Simply, it consists of a key word or phrase for each rule to identify what the rule is about. The rule above contains important elements which can be identified and listed. These are 'raining' and 'take an umbrella'. Thus the rule dictionary will contain two items:

raining 658
umbrella, take 658

The dictionary can be stored alphabetically or in related groups of items, each group alphabetic, or stored in both ways at once. As the system builder creates more rules so more items are added to the rule dictionary. The shell will prompt the builder to add new rules to the dictionary as they are entered. Eventually the rule dictionary is a mirror image of the rules. Anyone familiar with a dictionary of quotations will recognise the format. The first half of the book (system) contains the quotes (rules), the second half contains the index (dictionary). If the reader requires a quote relating to a keyword they refer to the index which tells them which quotes contain the keyword. Similarly, someone searching for a rule will search the rule dictionary looking for the key word, or words, and the dictionary will give the rule number, or numbers, containing the word, or words. This works in much the same way as a book index except, of course, we can utilise the power of the computer. The simplest method of search is to manually scan the dictionary to find the word, read across to find the rule number and then search the rules for the rule with the right number. Much better, of course, if the computer does the work like this:

> Do you want to find a rule? **Yes**
>
> What is a keyword in the rule? **rain**
>
> The rule containing the word rain is:
>
> Rule 658: If it is raining then take an umbrella
>
> Would you like to alter this rule?

It may be that you are not absolutely certain about the word you are looking for, in which case the system will prompt you to search the dictionary:

> Would you like to scan the dictionary? **Yes**
>
> Would you like to scan the whole dictionary or just one area? **Whole**
>
> Press return to move through the dictionary.
>
> When the keyword is highlighted on the screen please press S for search.

The usefulness of the dictionary depends upon the initial effort put into creating it. The time taken to create it will be well spent if subsequent access is easy, simple and accurate. It should be possible to locate all rules with particular words, even though they may not contain the exact word, by using synonyms, for example, shower and rain. Having identified the relevant rule then the necessary changes or modifications can be made not just to the rule but also to the associated help and even the dictionary entry itself. As knowledge bases grow, so direct access to the rules becomes slower and more tedious. The same is not true for a rule dictionary. The words in the dictionary are sorted and indexed alphabetically. Finding a key word, even in a large dictionary, is a relatively fast process. Try driving round the streets looking for somebody and then looking them up in a telephone directory!

CHANGING OTHER PARTS OF THE SYSTEM

Whilst it is likely that the knowledge in a domain will change, leading to changes in the knowledge base and hence the rules, it is also likely that other components of the rules will change. Whilst the numbers are unimportant in the sense that they are for locating rules only, it is reasonable not to change the numbers. However, the related help may be changed for several reasons. It is possible that the original help is ambiguous or limited and needs extending. Alternatively, the user may wish to augment the help with further explanation based on experience. Clearly it is better for subsequent users if they have more detailed knowledge of the rule, who wrote it, how it works, why it is relevant, how it has worked in the past, what it contributes to the system, how reliable it has been, or even on what occasions—date, time—and context it was invoked. As expert systems grow in complexity, they will be able to handle more help, more updates and more user contributions.

SYSTEM DOCUMENTATION

Any computer system will need updating and amending as time goes on. Despite this obvious need, suppliers of applications and packages have been reluctant to give the necessary support and tools for this to happen easily, without major upheaval. Nowhere is this more true than in the provision of documentation or supportive material. At best such material is scant, unreadable and largely irrelevant; at worst it is non-existent. There are many reasons for this sad state of affairs. Firstly, people who develop computer software are very much at the vanguard of development. It is very exciting producing software to do clever things. It is less exciting to produce a book on how to use it. Secondly, some of the people developing packages are illiterate. They may produce endless computer code to run a computer but ask them to produce a few words in good English about how to use it and they are beaten. Finally, any producer is anxious to get their product on the shelf of the shop so that it will sell as quickly as possible.

This is particularly true for computer software (and also hardware) where developments are so rapid that new products appear daily. Hardly has a new product appeared than we have the mark two or Plus version. The time available to market the product leaves little time for the niceties of writing manuals or sets of instructions.

However, the world is changing. As computers become cheaper and smaller, so they start to appear on the desk of the user. As the software packages become bigger, that is, more powerful, more interactive, and more friendly, so they are used by more people, known as end users. A large number of end users have not had formal training in computer technology. This has triggered something of a revolution. Software producers now produce supportive documentation, written, one suspects, by literates brought in for the purpose and not by the computer programmers.

Never mind, at least the suppliers are beginning to realise that the system will be used by non-experts who require intelligible help and advice. However, even now there are differences in the quality of help between packages, that is shells, and applications. Further the quality varies between suppliers. The more established and expensive a product the better the supporting material is likely to be. The cheaper and more prototypic the product the less help you are likely to get. What sort of help can you expect?

THE SHELL

When the system arrives in its box it will be unusable. The first thing the potential user must do is set up the package to run on their computer. This is not as easy as it may seem. Does the package have a manual giving instructions that are clear and concise? It is interesting to note that the supplier of what was considered to be one of the worst packages in terms of user friendliness has learnt the lesson and the latest version of the package now arrives with four manuals: getting started, learning, using and advanced topics.

After you have found your way around the package you may wish to use an example application before setting up your own. The supporting material should include examples of applications showing not only the range and versatility of the package but also highlighting problem areas and how to perform more complex tasks.

So far we have discussed supporting material in the form of a handbook or instructions. However, growing in importance as end users become system developers is the advent of on-screen help. Again the suppliers of poorly documented software have learnt the lesson and now provide so much available help on the screen that manuals may become obsolete. A good shell will have the screen clearly laid out so that you know exactly what you are doing at anytime. If you are stuck or confused you should have instant help facility to give advice, examples or further instuctions and then take you back to whatever you were doing. As the memory capacity of computers increases, so more and more space will be devoted to help and proportionately less to the actual package. The quality of on-screen help for most packages is exceptional and light years ahead of the screen displays only a few years ago.

USER SUPPORT

Whilst manufacturers and suppliers have improved their products almost beyond recognition, the end user has yet to catch up. The introduction of end user computing has not been paralleled with a similar improvement in end user skills. Often applications are developed using databases or spreadsheets, and, in the future, expert systems, which are without structure or documentation. Expediency has won its battle against husbandry. Many systems do not have sufficient back-up systems in the event of software or hardware failure. So what should a user do to support a developed expert system application?

Anybody implementing an expert system application must train potential users how to use it. Whilst an expert system is friendly and will provide help and explanation when asked, any user must be able to find their way around the system without wasting time and effort. An introduction to users explaining what the system is, how it works and its limitations, will be rewarded by the improved use made of the system.

PRODUCING DOCUMENTATION

Writing documentation, like writing a report or a book, is easier if you follow a defined series of stages. Firstly, consider your target audience. Who are you writing for? How much do they know already? How much jargon will they understand? Once you have some understanding of your audience you can plan the documentation, using a top down approach. Begin with an overall view of what you are producing and then look at the detail. What will the overall contents be? How can these be divided into meaningful smaller parts or chapters? Can chapters be further divided into smaller meaningful chunks that can be easily absorbed? Having determined content you can consider how best to present the material. Always use a variety of media: the written word, pictures and cartoons if possible. Choose a suitable format. An obvious choice is A4 but what about A5 or a fold-out? Instructions for using a system are best on cards that a potential user can keep by their computer. Having determined the contents, you need to consider structure. Make sure the material is logically organised. Give enough information to get people started early in the document and go into fine detail later.

Having produced a draft version you should let users comment on your contents, structure and style. Take notice of their comments even if they disagree with what you thought was brilliant material. Once the comments have been incorporated the final version can be polished and produced. This version could include a glossary of technical terms and a list of key words that will form an index. Once published, any documentation should be monitored to identify who is using it; does it do the job for which it was written and does it need revising? One final thought on documentation. Any work you produce, a manual, a users' guide, an application, will have a label. Ensure that you use labels that are meaningful now and in the future. 'Document MESUG : 260586' might mean someting at the moment but in a fews weeks, or even days, will you recognise it as 'MYCIN Expert System Users' Guide Version: 26 May 1986' The same principle applies to computer files, knowledge bases and anything else you produce.

One example of necessary documentation is a manual for an expert system application. All applications will require a manual. This will not be a day-to-day reference work but a complete analysis of the application. The manual should include a listing of the rules used in the knowledge base and an indication of their source. In addition the manual should list assumptions used in developing the application and how these may be reflected in the working of the system. The manual should also include the timescale of development and the limits of the knowledge with some indications of where future developments will occur. With this level of documentation the problems of updating should be reduced. Future developers should be able to trace the historical development of the application.

Any application will require a day-to-day reference or users' guide which explains how to use the system. The users' guide should cover the whole range of topics from 'How to switch on the machine' to 'What to do if smoke appears from the back of the computer', at least, 'What to do if the computer fails to work'. The user guide should direct users to sources of help in the event of either hardware or software failure.

In addition to the manuals, any application will have on-screen help. Probably this will be provided as part of the system shell although there is some scope for the developer to add things on the screen. This help is additional to help given during interrogation of the rules and should make the system easier to use. It may include an on-screen facility to print the complete interrogation of the system. This may seem obvious and straightforward but such a facility is not always included although it is useful. Other things on screen include what to do next, what to do if you want to quit and what to do if the system fails completely or locks up (which means that the computer will not respond to anything entered at the keyboard). All these things are self evident to computer experts but are less obvious to others without a degree in computer science.

EXTENDING THE EXISTING SYSTEM

There are two ways for a system to grow. Firstly, it will grow when more rules are added as knowledge is extended. Secondly, it will grow when rule sets are merged together, for example, the rules relating to one product range may be combined with the rules relating to another. To maintain such growing systems requires good housekeeping by keeping rules partitioned and also ensuring the rule dictionary is updated. However, problems will still arise. The shell may have a limit to the number of rules it can handle. The limit may be small, say 100, or very large, say several thousand, a limit unlikely to be reached.

Of more immediate concern is the speed of the system. As the system increases in size so the inference engine will access more and more rules. Unless the package is well written in a fast language the time taken by the computer to respond will get longer and longer. Eventually it becomes unbearable with the user able to have lunch while the computer makes up its mind what to do next. There is a wide variation in the speed of packages, depending on their level of sophistication and the language in which they are written.

As systems grow in size and the number of rules increases, so the possibilities of failure increase. Any change in quantity may affect the inherent quality. It is more difficult to manage larger systems. There will be problems of testing, documenting and updating any system as it grows. To avoid these difficulties it is better to approach any system in a modular way, that is, divide the application into smaller parts and develop, test and document each of these in turn. The final system will bring parts which will have been tried and tested individually. All that remains is to ensure that the parts fit together. Any rules that are common should use consistent nomenclature. Similarly, any variables used should have names that are consistent. Finally, the documentation should be extended to include the whole system with no gaps. Any adaptation or extension to an application will involve thorough testing and changes to the relevant documentation.

SECURITY

Paradoxically, having spent considerable time and effort putting your expert knowledge into an expert system to make it accessible to other people, the next step is to ensure that other people do not access that knowledge. In other words, making the knowledge secure. Modern computers make widespread access to information and knowledge bases a reality but this in turn opens up your system to all. There are two aspects to security, confidentiality and integrity. It may be that you want to restrict access to your system. Any application developed should give advantages to your organisation. Such benefits will also be useful to your competitors. Maintaining confidentiality means making the knowledge available but only to those people with a legitimate right to access it. On the other hand, maintaining integrity means keeping the knowledge base intact without loss or corruption so that the users can use it with confidence. Any system will require hardware, software and people. We will consider the security implications for all three.

HARDWARE

Potential users of computer systems are concerned that the equipment, that is, the hardware, will breakdown and thereby render the system useless. Such concern stems from our use of mechanical or electromechanical gadgets, such as our motor cars which may have been unreliable. Computers are very reliable. A computer from a reputable manufacturer should rarely breakdown. Like a hi-fi system, if it works for the first fortnight it will work forever.

What is likely to go wrong is not the electronics but the mechanical parts such as disk drives, printers and keyboards. It is worthwhile having contingency plans so that in the event of hardware failure your system will continue to work. The simplest but expensive solution is to have a duplicate set of identical hardware so that if one computer or printer fails you can use another. This solution is costly and you may consider it to be excessively cautious. It may be sufficient for you to have access to another machine in the event of hardware failure. As personal computers become more widespread so the problems of back-up hardware diminish. If your expert system application runs on a personal computer, chances are there are several other such computers in the organisation, one of which you can use. Nonetheless, it is worthwhile thinking about a maintenance contract to ensure that any hardware failure is put right as soon as possible thus avoiding prolonged use of other peoples' machines. As computer costs fall we may see organisations buying an extra personal computer as a spare machine, kept just for emergencies.

Personal computers are becoming widespread. Given their size and cost we can put them anywhere and everywhere. One word of caution. They may be robust but there are limits to their tolerance. They do not like extremes of temperature, dirt, smoke and other nasties. They do need to be treated with some respect. Unlike other office equipment that plug into the mains, personal computers do like a regular mains supply. If your location has fluctuacting power you may need to install correcting equipment to ensure the continued working of your computer and hence your expert system application.

SOFTWARE

Your software, including expert system shells and applications, are stored on floppy disks. The originals should be kept as masters, clearly labelled as such and stored in a safe place, preferably remote from the actual work area. Before being locked away, take working copies of each disk, again clearly labelled, for every day use. After initial copies are taken the master disks should never see the light of day, except in the event of further copies being needed bacause of some failure of the working copies. It is possible that your system uses a hard disk, in which case you should copy all the floppy disks onto the hard disk and then lock away the floppies for safe keeping in the same way.

Having looked after the physical side of disks, what about their contents? You may want to restrict access to certain knowledge bases. This can be done by using passwords, physical keys known as *dongles* and other more sophisticated devices, such as fingerprints. Detailed discussion of such devices is beyond the scope of the present book. Suffice it to say that security systems are available to restrict access to software. If you value you expert system then protect it. You need to protect software not just against prying eyes but also against damage, accidental or otherwise. Someone changing your knowledge base without you knowing could be potentially more dangerous than a rival organisation getting hold of a copy. You should ensure as far as possible that only authorised people have access to the knowledge. There are different levels of security. You can create a system which allows some people to interrogate the knowledge base, whilst others will be allowed full access to update and modify the knowledge base. Your choice of an expert system shell should take into account your particular needs for security.

In addition to the disk copies, you may have full listings on paper of the rules and perhaps even interrogations of an application. These should be kept securely and any copies not required should be shredded and dumped.

PEOPLE

The third requirement of a system is the people to run it. Generating an expert system assumes that the expert will not be around when it is used. The absence of the expert is almost built into the system. However, other people are less dispensable. What about the person who operates the computer, the knowledge base engineer, the knowledge base administrator? If they leave, retire or die can they be replaced? Is there somebody else in the organisation with the necessary skills and experience? If one of your employees leaves to work for a rival organisation will they take your knowledge base with them? Do your contracts clearly define ownership of intellectual property?

To maintain the hardware, update the software but neglect the users is courting disaster. Modern computers are easier to use but they still require training and practice. It is in your long term interests to maintain a workforce that is highly trained, motivated and loyal.

SUMMARY

In a perfect world it would be possible to build a computer system that would remain for all time. It would always run perfectly without need for update or improvement. Unfortunately this is not the case. We live in an ever changing world, perhaps we humans need the change. This continual change means we must be able to update and change our expert systems. This chapter started by looking at the reasons for change. It went on to consider the people involved in an expert system and considered why each will want to change the system in some way. Discussed in detail was the need for good documentation of the shell and the application to ensure that any system is used fully and effectively and can be updated and modified when necessary. This chapter considered the need to extend the system and the limits that may be reached. Finally, it looked at the important area of security of hardware, software and people.

6
An Example Knowledge Base

INTRODUCTION

In the preceding chapters we have looked at the stages in developing and using an expert system application. It may be helpful to look at a complete example of a real expert system. The example given below, 'Savings Adviser', was developed using Guru. Whilst there are differences between shells, notably in the way the rules are created, the example gives a general indication of the structure of an expert system application. The savings adviser is not large, the knowledge base has only nine rules, but it shows the constituent parts of a knowledge base. Of course, having created this working prototype it would be possible to extend the rules to include other factors.

THE PROBLEM

Imagine that we are being asked to set up a system to give advice to people about what they should do with their savings. We know there are rules which give three possibilities. We can advise they put all their money in savings, they put all their money in stocks or they split their money between the two. To help them decide which is the best option we need to have certain information about their personal and financial circumstances. This example handles numbers. We need to know the person's income, how much they have saved and how many dependents they have. This example also handles a logical item: is it true or false that the person's future income is steady? All these items or variables can be determined from the person making the enquiry. Other variables can be deduced by the expert system using the information given by the user. These are the level of income needed and an indication of whether or not the person has enough income and savings. The expert system will fire the rules according to the information given and give the relevant advice.

THE VARIABLES

Variables are the constants within a rule, for example, 'savings' and 'dependents'. Within one consultation of the expert system the variables have the same values. However, these values may vary in subsequent consultations. A complete list of variables for our problem is given below. Each variable has a name and a label. Each label provides additional information about its variable.

If the user is required to input a value for the variable, there will be a 'FIND' statement which gives the question to be asked and the variable that is being asked for. The format of the answer is determined by the input statement, num means it will be a number, 'dd' means two digits, str means it will be a string of characters and 'u' means one character which will be converted to uppercase.

```
VAR:   ADVICE
       LABEL:   The advice given

VAR:   GOODINCOME
       LABEL:   Income is good

VAR:   GOODSAVE
       LABEL:   Savings are good

VAR:   NEEDINCOME
       LABEL:   Income needed

VAR:   INCOME
       LABEL:   Current income
       FIND:    output " "
                input income num with \
                "What is your annual household income?"

VAR:   SAVINGS
       LABEL:   Current savings
       FIND:    output " "
```

```
                input savings num with \
                "How much do you have in savings?"

VAR:  STEADY
      LABEL:    Income is steady
      FIND:     output " "
                input steady str using "u" with \
                "Can you expect a steady income over the next year?
                (y/n)"
                steady = (steady = "Y")

VAR:  DEPENDENTS
      LABEL:    Number of dependents
      FIND:     output " "
                input dependents num using "dd" with \
                "How many dependents do you have? "
```

THE RULES

The logic of Savings Adviser is fairly simple. If the person has enough money they can risk stocks, too little money they are advised to use a regular savings scheme and if they fall between the two extremes they should split the money. We need to create rules that determine whether the level of savings is sufficient, see rules 8 and 9. You will observe that dependents are a drain on resources! We then need to establish the level of salary, again considering the number of dependents, rule 7, and whether it is sufficient and steady, rules 4, 5 and 6. Finally, we can give advice based on both savings and income, rules 1, 2 and 3.

The rules are divided into four parts, the rule number, the premise (the 'if' statement), the conclusion (the 'then' statement) and a reason. The reason will be displayed to the user in a 'How and Why' questioning. In addition to the four main parts Guru has secondary elements for each rule, which are not relevant here. A complete rule as it would appear on the screen, including the four main parts and additional information, is shown in Figure 9. The complete rule set is:

```
RULE: R1
      IF:         not goodsave
      THEN:       advice = "savings"
      REASON:     If the client does not have enough in savings,
                  the advice is to put all the money in savings.
```

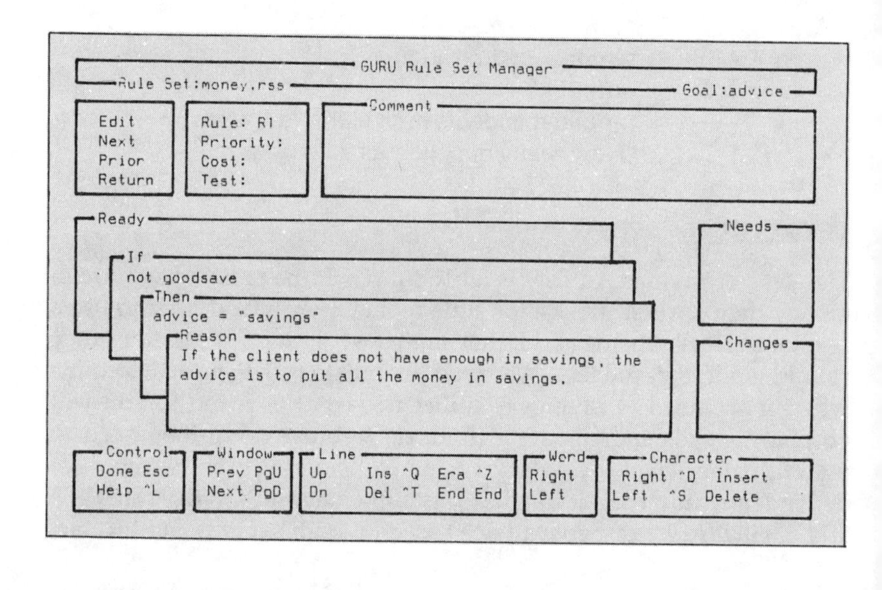

Figure 9: *An Example Rule in Guru*

RULE: R2
IF: goodsave and not goodincome
THEN: advice = "split"
REASON: If the client has sufficient savings, but not a good income, then the advice is to split the money between stocks and savings.

RULE: R3
IF: goodsave and goodincome
THEN: advice = "stocks"
REASON: If the client has a good income and enough in savings, then the advice is to invest in stocks.

RULE: R4
IF: not steady
THEN: goodincome = false
REASON: If the income for the next year is not steady, then it is not good income.

RULE: R5
IF: income <= needincome
THEN: goodincome = false
REASON: If the income is less than that needed by a family of this size, then it is not a good income.

RULE: R6
IF: steady and (income > needincome)
THEN: goodincome = true
REASON: To have a good income, the client's employment must be steady.

RULE: R7
IF: known("dependents")
THEN: needincome = 15 000 + (dependents * 4000)
REASON: If we know the number of dependents, then the needed income is £15 000 plus £4000 times the number of dependents.

RULE: R8
IF: savings > (5000 * dependents)
THEN: goodsave = true
REASON: If savings is greater than £5000 per dependent, then it is sufficient savings.

```
RULE: R9
      IF:        savings <= (5000 * dependents)
      THEN:      goodsave = false
      REASON:    If savings is less than £5000 per dependent, then
                 it is not sufficient savings.
```

THE INS AND OUTS

The inference engine uses the variables to execute the rules and provide the advice. It would appear that all that is required is the variables and rules but that is not the case. Any expert system developed using Guru has four sections: the rules, the variables, the initial conditions and the completing conditions. The initial and completing conditions provide the means for interacting with the rules, that is, the user interface. Additionally, the initial conditions determine the way the inference engine will work through the rules.

THE INITIAL CONDITIONS

The initial conditions set up the way the system will work. For example, Guru can assign different levels of certainty, and these are assigned at the beginning.

e.tryp = "e" *this condition tells the inference engine to evaluate the premise's conditions of each rule each time one of its unknown variables becomes known via backward chaining*
e.rigr = "m" *this condition tells the inference engine to stop considering rules as soon as the goal variable has a value, in this example: advice = "savings"*
e.lstr = 80 *the maximum length of inputs is 80 characters*
e.deci = 0 *no digits after the decimal points*

advice = unknown)
goodsave = unknown)
goodincome = unknown)
income = unknown) *sets up all variables as*
savings = unknown) *unknown at the start of each*
steady = unknown) *enquiry session*
needincome = unknown)
dependents = unknown)
clear *clears the screen*

```
at 2,28 output "Savings Adviser"   puts the title on the screen
output ""; output""                outputs two blank lines under the title
```

THE COMPLETING CONDITIONS

Having gone through the enquiry it is necessary to define the Completing Conditions to give the advice to the user. The Conditions test the goal and determine the display of the response based on a series of 'case statements' which are themselves like rules, for example, if advice=stocks then output 'You should invest the full amount in stocks'. The full Completing Conditions are:

```
output ""; output ""    outputs two blank lines
output "Based on the given information:"  opening line
output ""               outputs a blank line

test advice             determines the advice and gives the relevant
                        comment for each case available
case "stocks":
    output "You should invest the full amount in stocks"
    break
case "savings":
    output "You should put the full amount into savings"
    break
case "split":
    output "You should split the money between stocks and savings"
    break
endtest

e.deci = 2      resets the number of decimal places to two
```

EXAMPLE ENQUIRIES

Once the rules, variables input and completion conditions ahave been entered into the computer using the editor facilities of Guru, the application can be compiled into a version that will run quickly and saved on a disk. The application can then be distributed and used. A typical interaction by a user is:

```
                SAVINGS ADVISER

How much do you have in savings?       6000
How many dependents do you have?       4
```

Based on the given information:
You should put the full amount into savings

The user responds to the questions to ascertain the value of the variables and the rules are fired until a conclusion is reached. This interaction is straightforward because only two rules are fired. When asked to explain the reasoning, Guru lists the rules fired. The reasoning given shows that because of a lack of savings, 'savings are good' is false and R1 is fired which gives the conclusion: 'You should put all the amount into savings'. The reasoning also shows in parenthesis the variables being considered by each rule. Rule 9, known as R9 uses (5), (8) and (3). The number of the variable is followed by its label, its current value and a certainty factor (cf). In this example we are certain of all the figures and so the certainty factor for all variable and advice is 100%. Guru can handle uncertainty and this would be reflected in the cf values.

Rule R9 (fired)
If savings are less than £5000 per dependent, then it is not sufficient savings.

(5)	Current savings.	6000	cf 100
(8)	Number of dependents.	4	cf 100
(3)	Savings are good.	false	cf 100

Rule R1 (fired)
If the client does not have enough in savings, the advice is to put all the money in savings.

(3)	Savings are good.	false	cf 100
(1)	The advice given.	savings	cf 100

If the responses are less straightforward, then more rules are fired. In the example below, the higher savings, lack of dependents and high, steady income lead a different path through the rules.

SAVINGS ADVISER

How much do you have in savings?	20 000
How many dependents do you have?	0
Can you expect a steady income over the next year? (y/n)	Y
What is your annual household income?	30 000

Based on the given information:

You should invest the full amount in stocks

The reasoning shows that rules 8, 7, 6 and 3 are fired to give the conclusion: 'You should invest the full amount in stocks'. The layout of the variable numbers, labels, value and certainty factor is the same as the previous example.

Rule R8 (fired)
If savings is greater than £5000 per dependent, then it is sufficient savings.

(6)	Current savings	2000	cf 100
(8)	Number of dependents	0	cf 100
(3)	Savings are good	true	cf 100

Rule R7 (fired)
If we know the number of dependents, then the needed income is £15 000 plus £4000 times the number of dependents.

(8)	Number of dependents	0	cf 100
(4)	Income needed	1500.00	cf 100

Rule R6 (fired)
To have a good income, the client's employment must be steady.

(7)	Income is steady	true	cf 100
(5)	Current income	30 000	cf 100
(4)	Income needed	15 000.00	cf 100
(2)	Income is good	true	cf 100

Rule R3 (fired)
If the client has a good income and enough in savings, then the advice is to invest in stocks.

(3)	Savings are good	true	cf 100
(2)	Income is good'	true	cf 100
(1)	The advice given	stocks	cf 100

In the examples above, the required numerical information is input by the user of the system. This need not be the case. Guru is an integrated package with built in spreadsheet, database, text processing, graphics and communication facilities. Rather than inputting all of the information, some could be taken from a relevant database or spreadsheet. As inflation increases, the amount of money required for dependents will increase. Such information could be extracted from a database. Taking the example one stage further, the expert system could call up information from data sources outside Guru, such as stock exchange figures, bank rate, the value of the dollar, etc. This up-to-date information could be used by the expert system to give excellent savings advice.

SUMMARY

This chapter described an example knowledge base, 'Savings adviser', and examples of interactions with reasoning. Whilst the example itself is, of necessity, small, it is complete. The adviser shows the constituent parts necessary to create a full application. The chapter concluded with a brief look at how such a system could be linked to external sources of data to provide up-to-date advice.

7
Examples of Applications

INTRODUCTION

Having reviewed what expert systems are, we can consider some real applications. As stated earlier, expert systems have not yet been recognised as a management tool, consequently there is not a large catalogue of existing applications. Add to this the specific nature of expert systems and the problem becomes even more difficult. If an expert system encapsulates the knowledge or expertise of an organisation, that organisation is hardly likely to make it public. Thus, comparatively few applications are actually reported in the literature. The defence agencies, perhaps foreseeing trends in the future, are restricting reporting on artificial intelligence and expert systems' developments. However, we know that applications have been developed and some of these have been made public. Even if the actual contents are hidden, developers are willing to talk about how far they have got in developing their system.

Surveys suggest that only large companies have taken expert systems on board for developing applications. They have the resources to give the necessary man months of time to develop a system and they can cope with the risk of failure. Even so, few of them have large scale working systems. On the other hand, small companies may well buy a shell to develop small applications or, more likely, buy an application for a specific purpose. In this chapter we look at large systems that have been developed generally for research purposes and, also, smaller scale applications that are in use today. These examples will give you an indication of what use expert systems can be in your environment.

EXAMPLES OF EXPERT SYSTEM APPLICATIONS

Whilst it is difficult identifying exactly where research and development are being carried out in the field of expert systems, we do know the types of application from surveys of users. Not surprisingly, the largest area of activity is in the field of medicine. There is an enormous body of knowledge relating to medical care which changes very slowly, making it ideal as a knowledge base for an expert system. The diagnosis of illness or disease is an interrogation of this knowledge base. Second to medicine, in its interest in expert systems, is the military. Again this is not unexpected. It is fair to argue that the military and the space programme are responsible for an enormous range of developments both in software and hardware. The computer industry itself, perhaps as part of an awareness campaign, is very active in developing applications in AI and, particularly, expert systems. The final major investor in such systems is the finance sector who are becoming more committed to technology and its use. Other areas of application include personnel, manufacturing and engineering, law, farming, real time systems, computer assisted learning (CAL) and information retrieval.

MEDICINE

Medicine is a rich hunting ground for expert systems. Health care uses an enormous amount of resources and any attempt at making it more effective and efficient is welcome. Further, the medical profession employs experts (consultants) who have spent a long time developing their knowledge and skills which will be lost to the profession when they retire. The very nature of medical diagnosis is an expert system, with a user digging through a knowledge base (forward chaining) to come up with an answer, that is, looking for a cure. Alternatively, the user looks back through a knowledge base (backward chaining) to find a cause, that is, to discover why this person rather than that person developed cancer. Finally, medical researchers, if not the practitioners themselves, are willing to use new technology to help in diagnosis and treatment.

The grandfather, and perhaps the originator, of the current approach to expert systems is MYCIN, a system developed at Stanford University in the mid 1970s to aid doctors in the selection of antibiotics for patients with severe infections. MYCIN has a knowledge base of about 500 rules and has demonstrated an ability to perform at the same level as experienced doctors. Although a research project and never implemented as a full working system, MYCIN is important because it spawned a generation of expert systems. MYCIN itself has been rewritten as TEIRESIAS and, subsequently, as an aid in the education of medical students called GUIDON.

EMYCIN was designed and written by Van Melle at Stanford. It is an inference engine based on the MYCIN system that can be used to create and interrogate a knowledge base. Although largely a research shell, it gave rise to KS 300 which in turn led to the development of M1, a commercially available shell. EMYCIN was used to develop PUFF, a system used to analyse pulmonary functions with a 90% success rate. PUFF, a comparatively small system, has been converted into BASIC to run on smaller computers.

Another early system worth mentioning is DENDRAL, which was developed to analyse mass spectral patterns to suggest the chemical structure of unknown compounds. DENDRAL is well tested, documented and currently in use. The third system, often quoted, is PROSPECTOR, a derivative of MYCIN, which is concerned with mineral exploration and drilling sites. Like MYCIN, PROSPECTOR has never been commercially used although it has formed the basis of further research by mineral and oil companies. PROSPECTOR has a knowledge acquisition system, KAS, which allows it to be used outside geology domains, rather like EMYCIN is a more generally applicable version of MYCIN. Incidentally, MYCIN also spawned RITA, Rand Intelligent Terminal Agent, an early programming system, which in turn spawned ROSIE, Rule-Oriented System for Implementing Expertise, a general purpose programming system for building expert systems. ROSIE has been used for developing legal applications, see below.

Two other specific medical systems are worth a mention. CASNET is a system to aid in the consultancy of patients with glaucoma. ONCOCIN is a system that recommends chemotherapy for cancer patients.

In addition to attempts at specific areas of diagnosis, researchers are striving to replicate the general practitioner who is confronted with a bewildering array of symptoms. In the United States one such attempt is INTERNIST-1 which undertakes diagnosis for all problems in internal medicine. INTERNIST-1 has achieved a degree of success, given the enormity of the problem, and a successor, CADUCEUS, is being developed. In the United Kingdom, Dr John Fox and a team at the Imperial Cancer Research Fund in conjunction with Oxford University Press have developed a prototype system for general practitioners called the Oxford System of Medicine (OSM). The system was developed using Props 2, like XI a derivative of ICRF's Props. OSM has four facilities: it will store patient records, it will store the text of medical books, it will assist with diagnosis and it will explain its behaviour.

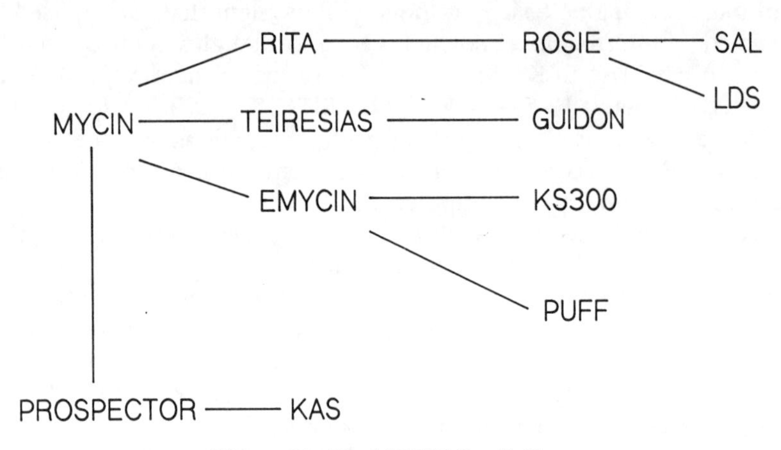

Figure 10: *The MYCIN Family Tree*

All these medical systems have two points in common. They are all attempting to embody human knowledge and they are all intended to help others make judgements based on this knowledge. They epitomise expert systems. Additionally, medical expert systems have had wide-ranging consequences for other applications. As Figure 10 indicates, the early, pioneering medical systems gave the impetus and often the software to develop further systems. The principles underlying MYCIN, the grandfather of expert systems, have permeated all other rule-based expert systems.

MILITARY

As they have developed in size and scope expert systems have been perceived as having a role to play in military applications. As such systems are developed and become real applications, rather than research projects, so the level of associated secrecy grows. Nonetheless, there are areas of application that are open to the public.

One such area of application is in the field of target recognition where the expert system identifies objects embodied in a panoramic scene. Current systems are able to categorise objects in particular ways but, with incomplete information, often fail to make valid recognitions. Using an expert system, an Automatic Target Recognition System should be able to take into account not just the parameters but also the context of the object, thus increasing the chances of recognition. This area of research has implications for non-military applications where recognising objects is important. Examples here range from using the system as part of a security system to object recognition as a part of quality control.

Another area of application is the development of intelligent, pilotless vehicles that have a full range of senses. Such vehicles need not be built to carry and protect a human and so will be smaller, lighter and more manoeuvrable. This is particularly beneficial for air going craft, including helicopters. Again, this area of research has implications for civilian applications such as remote inspection machines that can be sent into environments inaccessible to humans.

COMPUTER INDUSTRY

As computers have developed, so the task of configuring systems has become increasingly more difficult. A personal computer system will consist of a box containing the processor, one or two disk drives, a VDU and a printer. Slightly more sophisticated systems may have a mouse and a modem or be networked, that is, linked to other computers. Putting such a package together causes few problems. However, developing large systems is not so straightforward. Here it is possible to specify endless combinations of processors, disk drives, back up memory, printers, plotters, interfaces and cables. Quite often a system would arrive on site and would not 'fit' together, simply because the component parts were incompatible or missing.

The way that systems are put together can be defined in a set of rules, which form the knowledge base of an expert system. The first and, perhaps, most famous system is the R1 system developed by DEC. This system, also known as XCON, was designed to aid DEC staff who are responsible for configuring systems based on Vax computers. It is reported that R1 has reduced the time taken to configure a system from 30 minutes to less than a minute. In addition, the system has saved thousands of pounds, since materials are utilised more effectively and fewer errors mean less delivery delays or materials returned.

DEC are not alone in developing expert systems for computer configurations. IBM, ICL, Nixdorf and Xerox have developed such systems. ICL, like other manufacturers has realised that computers must be seen to be working, have also developed an expert system using a shell REVEAL which will help managers forecast usage of ICL's VME machines. The system is called VME Capacity Management System (VCMS) and is aimed directly at data processing managers.

FINANCE

There are several possible areas of application in the finance area, since many financial decisions are based on a series of rules. One such area of application is in the field of ELCs, export letters of credit. This system developed by Helix, using Expert Edge, uses a knowledge base of some 250 rules to search for, and evaluate, discrepancies which may lead to payment on the credit being refused. 'Letter of Credit Adviser' will handle the six main documents relating to export credit: drafts, transport documents, invoices, certificates of origin, packing lists and insurance documents. Using an expert system shell to create and interrogate the knowledge base allows any user to add rules to the system to cover particular contingencies.

In addition to the above system, there are several other applications in the finance area. One such application is a package called Auditor which aids auditors in their estimation of uncollectible accounts receivable. Another application is TAXADVISOR, developed on a large mainframe computer using EMYCIN, which assists lawyers with tax planning for clients with large estates, including insurance purchases, retirement actions, wealth transfer and will modification. Other applications include a system using ACLS to evaluate bad debts and a system to aid bank auditors to evaluate the collectibility of loans using the shell M1.

The possibility of expert systems in finance is reflected in the interest shown by Alvey. One of the user clubs instigated by the Alvey Directorate is ALFEX, a consortium of twenty-five banks and financial consultants who are pursuing the application of expert systems in the financial sector. There are two systems currently being developed. The first is a system for assessing fire risk in the clothing trade and the second is a system to evaluate decisions to buy and sell in equity investment.

PERSONNEL

Personnel departments make decisions about prospective or current employees based on a set of often ill-defined rules. Several attempts have been made at creating a knowledge base to help personnel managers carry out their tasks more effectively.

Taking a career path of an individual, the first thing he or she must do is submit an application form and be selected for interview. Whilst going through application forms may not seem too onerous the problem is overwhelming when an organisation has several hundred applications to consider. This will be the case for such companies as employment agencies. Helix, using Expert Edge, have developed a package called CV Filter which uses objective and subjective criteria to assess suitability of candidates. The system can be set up incorporating criteria determined by the relevant manager and it can be used subsequently by less costly staff in the organisation.

Having identified the short list, the next stage is to interview candidates and make a final selection. ICL using their Adviser shell have produced a package called Staff Interview Adviser. This application guides managers through the considerations they should make before interviewing. After the interviews, the Adviser helps managers assess each applicant and record details of interviews in a manner which is consistent.

Following appointment, the details of employees will be entered into the company's database. Since this is personal information it will be covered by the Data Protection Act. Managers can receive guidance on the Act from two different expert sytem applications. The first is the Data Protection Adviser, developed by Intelligent Environments using their shell Crystal. The second is the Data Protection Act Adviser, developed by Helix using their shell Expert Edge.

Having been appointed, a new employee may take time off because of illness. Expertech have produced a system to help managers understand and apply the DHSS's regulations on Statutory Sick Pay (SSP). The application, called Clarifying Statutory Sick Pay Regulations was developed using Expertech expert system shell XI. The system comprises a set of six linked knowledge bases, which gives some indication of the complexity of the regulations.

The final stage in the employment life cycle is dismissal. Again there is an expert system application to help managers, this time through the labyrinth of employment legislation. Called Employment Law: Clarifying Dismissal, the system was also developed by Expertech using their shell XI.

MANUFACTURE AND ENGINEERING DESIGN

Some manufacturing industries are keen to exploit the potential of computer technology using the variety of packages available for computer assisted design (CAD), computer assisted manufacturing (CAM) and, more recently, computer integrated manufacture (CIM). These systems are designed to help production engineers convert an idea for a product into a manufactured article. The process involves creating drawings of the product, specifying the materials and determining the manufacturing process such as milling or turning. Each stage requires a wealth of knowledge and experience, some of which can be encapsulated in an expert system. One such system is DClass, written in Fortran and developed at Brigham Young University. DClass can be used for the classification of products, estimating costs and process planning.

Another system that aids in the planning process is EDS, an Engineering Decision Support System. This application was developed by the British Hydromechanics Research Association, using an expert system shell also developed by them called Chloe. EDS is based on one of the largest knowledge bases in Europe that contains information about the choice of control valves in a piping system. Whilst such choices may seem mundane, the design of piping systems is expensive and mistakes can be costly. Following an interrogation phase, the system produces a list of recommended valves with associated preferences. It also gives a full specification and the reasons for the choices it has made, thus enabling designers to complete systems without constant recourse to a valve expert.

LAW

In the United States several systems have been developed in the legal area. More attention has been given to technology and the law than in the UK where lawyers have been slower to identify and capitalise on the benefits. There are a few legal systems relating to particular legislation in the UK, for example, data protection and unfair dismissal, but little general expert system support for the legal profession. In America two applications have been developed using ROSIE, the system developed from EMYCIN. The first is a legal decision making system, LDS. This system calculates defendant liability, case worth and an equitable settlement amount. The knowledge in LDS is based on legal texts, legislation and the legal knowledge of law professors, claims adjusters and both plaintiff and defence lawyers. The expertise covers product liability, including negligence and liability legislation, as well as the principles and strategies used by legal experts.

The second application using ROSIE is SAL, a rule-based system for evaluating asbestos claims, The System for Asbestos Litigation. SAL considers just one disease, asbestosis, and one class of plaintiffs, insulators. Nonetheless, the application, which contains approximately 400 rules, is a good example of how expert systems can help handle legal problems. Estimates of asbestos exposure, in the US, are in the order of 20 million with over 200 thousand related deaths, the potential litigation is enormous. SAL should help speed the litigation process by analysing asbestos claims and producing dollar values for the cases. The system, currently a research vehicle, will be used by judges, law firms and insurance companies. It can be used to evaluate settlements and also to train new personnel in this area.

There are several other expert system applications in the legal area. These include: CORPTAX, which assists lawyers with problems of federal corporate taxation focusing on the tax treatment of stock redemption; DSCAS, which helps contractors analyse the legal aspects of differing site conditions, determining when additional expenses can be allowed; EXPERT TAX SYSTEM, which provides tax inspectors with advice about apportionment of a corporation's income by applying knowledge concerning current tax legislation, and TAXADVISOR mentioned above.

The above examples may be considered rather more in the finance area than in the legal area. Nonetheless they do illustrate some of the possibilities of applying expert systems to law. There are obvious applications for expert systems to be applied to the law, for example, to help interpret the law in the context of a particular question. However, there are other possible areas of application that are less obvious. These include: organising case information, estimating case value, developing strategies for handling cases, monitoring legal databases, retrieving knowledge from such databases and producing legal documents by selecting and organising text according to users' needs. Given the most expensive aspect of the law is the lawyer's (expert's) time, it is likely that expert systems will be exploited to make the maximum use of such time. Of course, this argument applies to all professionals, including accountants, architects, surveyors and bankers. Expert systems could be used effectively in all areas to free professionals' time.

FARMING

Farmers have managed to increase yields several times over despite an actual reduction in the acreage of arable land given over to crops. This has been brought about partly by the use of chemicals such as nutrients and pesticides. However, as the range of chemicals increases so the farmers face a more difficult task of selection. ICI, a large producer of chemicals and, therefore, involved in the problem, have developed an expert system application to give advice to farmers. The system is called Wheat Counsellor and it was developed using the shell Savoir from ISI, itself partly owned by ICI.

Wheat Counsellor is based on a generalised system called Counsellor that will be used to generate systems for barley and oil seed rape. An interesting aspect of the Counsellor system is that it is held on a central mainframe and farmers access the information via a viewdata service called Grapevine. The knowledge base not only has information about diseases and their causes and cures, it can also access a database which contains information about the farms that have access to the system. This information reduces the amount of interrogation needed for each enquiry. A further feature of the system is its ability to access a video disk to show farmers examples of the things asked by the system. Following the interrogation Wheat Counsellor recommends a course of action. Whilst this system is centred around crop diseases, the model can be applied to fault analysis in any context, with users able to call up for advice and suggested remedies.

REAL TIME SYSTEMS

So far there has been less emphasis on real time systems compared with those systems that are used for ad hoc advice and consultation. This does not mean that such applications are not valid and effective, rather it indicates the embryonic state of expert system applications. Nonetheless, there are systems in existence and several in the course of development. It is expected that real time expert systems will not have the shortcomings of their human counterpart who overlook information, are inconsistent, are slow and are deluged in a crisis.

One obvious area of application is in the control of continuous process systems which require twenty-four hour monitoring. Escort, developed by PA Computers and Telecommunications, is a real time system that advises on oil platform process control. Another real time application is YES/MVS a system developed by IBM to assist operators with the MVS operating system on IBM computers. YES/MVS not only gives advice but also takes over some of the operations normally performed by the operator.

Real time applications used in process control should improve productivity, reduce wastage and eliminate the danger of human error thus reducing the risk of another Bhopal or Chernobyl.

COMPUTER ASSISTED LEARNING

The ability to put information together in frames and then use an expert system to access these frames opens up an exciting avenue of development. As in Wheat Counsellor, an expert system can access sound and text, still photographs and video and it will respond to a user's need by pursuing different avenues through the knowledge base. We have assumed that such applications are set up to augment the knowledge of the user. Alternatively, we can set up an application to transfer the knowledge to the user. Such an approach can be used for training employees, updating the sales team on the company's products and providing an interactive system for customers about the product range.

Using an expert system gives an opportunity to convey information. However, it does more than just present information to the user. The system asks questions and the user responds. This interaction can be used to test the user's understanding of the information. Built into the knowledge base there can be rules which measure the understanding of the individual. In this way expert systems can be used to present information, but, also, they can be used for diagnostic purposes to see what further information should be presented. How the user responds to particular questions will determine their path through the knowledge base. Beginners may be expected to work right through the knowledge base whilst those with more knowledge or experience will follow a shorter, quicker route. In this way computer assisted learning will be responsive to individual learning needs.

Paradoxically, creating centralised training packages, using expert systems, makes them more accessible, not less. Any package developed, such as an induction training, health and safety update, etc. can be used within a distance learning environment to disseminate the information as widely as possible. Linking the various parts of information technology together: expert systems, interactive graphics, communications and cheap accessible terminals, gives a wonderful opportunity for advances in training methods.

INFORMATION RETRIEVAL

Imagine you are working on a problem and you need information about quarterly sales. You know roughly what you want and where to look. To determine your exact requirements you will go through a question and answer session with yourself. These questions will pinpoint your information requirements and identify where in your organisation the information is held. As organisations grow, so the amount of available information grows. The problem is compounded by computer-based information systems that hold masses of information. The personal computer on your desk will access not just your personal database, not just the central database of the organisation but also the commercial databases that you subscribe to in the hope and belief that the information they give you is relevant, useful and accessible. How do you find your way around all this information? One solution is to use an expert system as a clever indexing system. Since we access the information by rules, for example, if we want the national sales figures then we look in the central database, we can create a knowledge base about our knowledge and make accessing so much easier.

SUMMARY

The advent of expert systems has led to a large number of promises with few actual results so far. There are comparatively few expert system applications available for inspection. Nonetheless, those that are available show some of the promise of future computer applications. The examples given above, whilst relating to particular areas such as medicine or farming , are relevant to other areas as well. Expert systems involve the creation of a knowledge base and the application of this knowledge to a particular problem. The principles involved can be universally applied. The experience gained from target recognition in military applications has implications for manufacturing. Similarly, the experience gained in medical diagnosis can be utilised in developing fault diagnosis systems in oil rigs. Expert system applications will be limited by imagination and not by technology.

8
Choosing a Shell

INTRODUCTION

As interest in expert systems grows, so the number of shells increases. A listing of available shells is given in Chapter nine, but what should a potential user take into account when trying to choose just one from such a wide choice. In this chapter we will consider some of the factors that will influence the purchasing decision. A checklist is given at the end of the chapter.

COMPUTER LANGUAGES

Expert system shells are written in a variety of computer programming languages, each with its particular strengths and weaknesses. In order to consider the relative merits of one language over another we need to distinguish between two types of computer language: imperative and assertional.

IMPERATIVE LANGUAGES

Imperative languages are written in the form of a list of commands that the computer is expected to carry out in the order prescribed by the programmer. Such a program may use data, but this data will not affect the program listing. A program to evaluate pay and overtime may use the number of hours worked by a person, but the program itself will remain in its original form so that if run again it will perform the identical task. To evaluate pay and overtime would require the following program, which is in outline form:

open employee file
look up first employee

multiply standard hours by hourly rate
establish number of overtime hours
multiply overtime hours by overtime rate
add standard and overtime pay
look up tax allowances
deduct tax allowances
evaluate tax due
deduct tax due
deduct all other deductions
add tax allowances
print pay slip
go to next employee
repeat until all employees have been paid

This example, whilst it is only an outline and not an actual program, gives an indication of the rote nature of imperative languages. All employees will be treated in an identical way, which is as it should be with pay and overtime!

The majority of languages currently in use are imperative, indeed, when we talk of learning a computer language we imply that we are learning the set of commands necessary to make it perform certain tasks.

There are several imperative languages such as BASIC, Pascal, Forth and PL1, but one in particular is worth a mention. C is an imperative language that has proved very popular with software developers writing expert system shells. C, like Pascal, is a structured language capable of handling a knowledge base but it is better for writing applications that interact with the user. Programs written in C run very quickly and make full use of the computer screen display.

ASSERTIONAL LANGUAGES

Assertional language programs do not consist of a series of commands, in fact, they may not be recognisible as programs at all. They are constructed in the same way that we collect information about the world. We do not think in an imperative way. Rather we see the world as a collection of objects and relationships, for example, employees work in department X. Here we have two objects: employees and department X and the relationship between them: works in. An assertional language will allow us to make assertions about the world and then manipulate and test these statements. Assertional languages can be sub-divided into two further categories: functional and logical languages.

FUNCTIONAL LANGUAGES

As the name suggests functional languages are designed to handle particular functions. There are several examples, one of the most important being LISP which is a language which has the ability to handle lists of entities. In the pay and overtime example, the entities, for example, the employees are an inherent part of the program. The advantage of a list processing language is it can easily add, remove, shuffle and reshuffle the items. Because the world is full of lists, LISP can imitate reality. For example, a queue of patients waiting for the doctor can be considered as a list of patients with names being continually added to the bottom and occasionally names being removed from the top. LISP is popular with the 'scruffies', mentioned in Chapter one, particularly in North America. It is one of the languages used for writing expert systems.

LOGICAL LANGUAGES

Logic is concerned with the validity of arguments. It is used to tell us whether given conclusions can be drawn from given premises. Such an organised approach is favoured by the 'neats', mentioned in Chapter one. A widely known method of logic is 'modus ponendo ponens', usually referred to affectionately as modus ponens. The argument runs:

All swans are white
This is a swan
Therefore it is white

This can be written in a universal form:

if P then Q, P therefore Q

This form relates directly to the rules of expert systems. Using modus ponens, we can use existing facts P to determine new facts Q. The logic can be expressed in the form of predicate calculus. The swan example would be written:

are (swans,white)

The objects, swans and white, are known as arguments, the relation, are, is known as the predicate.

There are languages developed, based on predicate calculus, for AI applications. The obvious example here is PROLOG (PROgramming in LOGic) which attempts to replicate the real world. An example of PROLOG, which puts arguments and predicates in a better order, could look like this:

> Smith works-for Hardings
>
> Hardings manufacture wheelbarrows
>
> x make z if x works-for y and y manufacture z
>
> Does Smith make wheelbarrows?
>
> YES

This example illustrates the different nature of an assertive language, compared with an imperative language. Using such a system of entities like employee, manager, department, etc., and relationships like works-for, make, etc., it should be possible to build up a whole framework of knowledge about a system, so that we can ask questions about the company.

The imperative languages have been with us for a long time. They will continue to be used for straightforward applications where the same thing must be done a lot of times, for example, evaluating a person's pay and overtime. However, the future perhaps lies in the computers ability to manipulate enormous amounts of information at the same time, so that it can make 'intelligent' judgments about the world. The Japanese have said that the language of the 80s will be PROLOG.

However, for the moment expert system shells are written in both imperative and assertional languages. PROLOG has yet to dominate although cheaper and faster versions are becoming available and will be used more widely. At the moment the choice is between the two. Suppliers of shells written in imperative languages claim rightly that they are fast and economical. On the other hand, assertional languages have an inherent structure suitable for AI applications. One inherent difficulty with assertional languages is their lack of availability on any machine other than a purpose built AI workstation, which has tended to be comparatively expensive. However, with improvements in technology it is possible to run LISP or PROLOG on normal business machines by adding a chip containing the ability to speak the language, known as 'LISP on a chip'. As we move toward a new generation of computers, the fifth generation, small computers have more processing power, run faster and can access larger memories. Small scale assertional languges are becoming available on personal computers. Eventually, the shells written in assertional languages will be as fast and as economical as those written in imperative languages. However, they will have the advantage of the built-in structure suitable for AI developments such as the ability to understand natural language, English.

FACTORS INFLUENCING THE PURCHASE OF AN EXPERT SYSTEM SHELL

HARDWARE

The advent of personal computers has changed the method for choosing a system. Previously, you chose software applications to run on your mainframe computer. Now the plethora of affordable personal computers and software packages has reversed the process. The important consideration now is to choose your software and then buy a computer to run it. This holds good for most of the shells listed in Chapter nine. Given the de facto standards imposed by IBM most software will run on IBM or IBM compatible machines. However, there are exceptions where software is written for a particular language not supported on an IBM machine or for a specific machine. If your organisation has implemented computer systems already, such as accounting, word processing or a data base, then it is sensible to choose an expert system that will run on existing hardware. If a new machine is purchased to run an expert system, it should be compatible with existing machines. Buying from one manufacturer, or at least retaining compatibility with one manufacturer, will reduce maintenance costs. In addition, it should ensure transferability of data between work stations. This will allow expert systems to access existing data such as personnel records, marketing breakdowns, running costs, etc.

COMPANY POLICY

If your organisation has formulated an information system strategy, there are likely to be constraints within which purchases must be made. Such restraints can relate to hardware, software, suppliers and even maintenance contracts. If there are expert systems currently in use, or, more likely, being developed, it is sensible to buy and use the same shell wherever possible. Like hardware, compatibility of software reduces costs and increases the chances of success with less dilution of resources.

HOME OR ABROAD

One particular consideration which may be laid down by the organisational policy is the decision to buy at home or abroad. Whilst the simplest argument for home purchase is to support local industry, there are other cogent arguments, such as the proximity of suppliers, the handiness of support, the number of fellow users in your area or even country. All of these may point to a restricted purchasing policy.

SIZE

Having narrowed down the field to a group of particular suppliers you can consider each individual shell. The first concern will be the package's ability to cope with the task in hand. Specifically, will the package handle the size of project? As your system grows, there may be an appreciable decline in response time as the inference engine crunches its way through the rule base. Editing and updating the rules becomes more difficult as systems grow larger. Some means of accessing the rules such as a rule dictionary is essential.

PERFORMANCE

The ability to handle large sets of rules quickly is one measure of performance for a system. There are others, such as the system's validity and reliability, terms covered in a previous chapter. How can we tell that an expert system is behaving correctly, going through the right rules and giving good advice? One answer is the use of standard tests to measure a system's performance. Just as there are bench marks for assessing the performance of more traditional packages, for example, one test is to time how long it takes for a computer to evaluate 100 square roots, perhaps we could have bench marks in the form of rule bases that test expert systems.

REGISTERD SOFTWARE

Unfortunately, not all software is of a reasonable calibre doing what it claims to do and reasonably priced. This is true of all types of packages and not just expert systems. Buying from a well established large supplier is likely to ensure success, but even so you can never be sure that the product is satisfactory. One suggestion to cope with the range of quality is to register software in some way, so that prospective purchasers can look for the seal of approval. This is a good idea but would be difficult to implement.

The first problem is to determine who should give the seal of approval. The obvious suggestion is self regulation within the industry but this is fraught with danger. Will the companies govern themselves or simply accept each others products in the knowledge that rejecting someone else's package could mean the demise of their own?

There could be legal constraints. It is unlawful for somebody to sell a product which will not do the job for which it was intended. This is fine if there is controversy over the suitability of a kettle which will not boil water, it is much more difficult to define legally the intended purpose of a software package that is intended to be used to create a myriad of applications beyond the control of the supplier.

A further suggestion is that a third party such as the NCC (National Computing Centre) should act as a watchdog, like the British Standards Institute. Again there are inherent problems with this suggestion, because the nature and role of software packages are difficult to define, unlike kettles, about which we have some agreement. Furthermore, producers of software are naturally reluctant to divulge the secrets of their packages which will have taken yeasrs to develop. Would an outside body be expected to judge the package or would they be allowed to disect in minute detail the workings of the package, thus exposing the secrets of the package? Until some form of control is imposed from within or without it is still 'caveat emptor'—let the buyer beware.

HELP

A major difference between shells is the quality of help given both in the supporting literature and also on the screen. As a general rule later versions of packages are better than earlier versions although they may not be fully tested and trouble free. The amount of time and effort to create the help systems around the core of the package to make it more usable will be reflected in the cost to the user.

SUPPORT

Users of any software occasionally run into difficulties. Whilst such traumas can be overcome by digging through the manual, trial and error and sometimes good luck, there are occasions when outside help is needed. A question you should ask about any software package is how much support is available from the supplier of the software. If you purchase certain packages, you will be given free training, maintenance support and hot line facilities, that is, the facility to telephone to discuss problems you are having. You may also get consultancy support from your supplier, but at a cost.

In addition to help from the original supplier you may want support from your own computer department. Make sure that they support your original purchase decision, they are more likely to give you help in the future if they were involved at the beginning.

Well established software packages and hardware have related user groups. These are collections of people interested in getting the most from their system. Usually they are not directly linked with the supplier. Thus they are able to bring pressure on the suppliers to improve, update or modify their products. Perhaps the measure of success of expert systems will be when independent user groups are set up and thriving.

EXISTING APPLICATIONS ON THE SYSTEM

The newer the package the more likely it is to be 'all singing and dancing' but with the disadvantage that it may not be fully tested. It is often better to buy the last version of a package which has a tried and tested user base that you can inspect and evaluate. It is worthwhile asking the supplier if there are applications in your area that you can visit. However, do not expect a rival company in the same line of business to be free and open with their expert system.

Reputable software houses who produce and supply packages will maintain compatibility wherever possible. If you have created a rule base using version one of a shell and the software supplier brings out version two which is faster, easier, provides more help, more graphics or whatever, it should be possible for you to pay a small premium, obtain version two and still use your rule base.

SECURITY

If you develop an expert system application, you will want to ensure that the contents are held secure and only accessible to legitimate users. Before purchasing a shell, read through the guidelines on security given in Chapter five. Compare the facilities available with each shell and determine which you need and which are desirable but not essential. The more widespread the application the more security you will require to maintain condfidentiality and integrity.

COST

Cost is the last thing to worry about when choosing a shell. Compared with the cost of the hardware, the development time, the user time and the cost of failure, the cost of the package is marginal. It is true to say that you get what you pay for in software. The price of a package can range from £50 to £50 000. Choose the package that will run on your hardware, will meet your needs and will produce a useful expert system.

LIMITATIONS WITH EXISTING SHELLS

Expert system shells are a recent addition to the range of software available. Consequently, these shells have limitations which become more apparent as their use becomes more widespread. Often the shell that you purchase is not the original version but is the second, third or fourth version of the product. Each version being an improvement on the one before. It is likely that the earlier versions were never marketed but were created solely for development purposes. There are several areas where development could take place.

Firstly, the method of acquiring knowledge is still rather a hit and miss affair. The knowledge acquisition facility within the shell should provide a suitable framework for the knowledge engineer to create a valid knowledge base. The shell itself should be intelligent enough to identify blind alleys, incomplete rules, inconsistencies and all the other potential errors in the knowledge base. Secondly, expert system shells should have built in test facilities which trace through the rules to prove that any knowledge base created is complete, valid and reliable. Thirdly, the explanation and help offered to the user should be more than a restatement of the rules. One major difference between expert systems and traditional programming techniques is the level of potential help. This help should be fully exploited.

There are two constraints on developments such as these. The first is our lack of understanding. It may be that we will never have an expert system shell that is fully self-testing because it is beyond the wit of man to devise such a shell. The second constraint is computing power, which we can influence. The advent of new, large, powerful, cheap computers will give the hardware necessary to produce the necessary software for smaller systems. The larger the shell, the more likely it is to have some of the facilities mentioned above. On the one hand software prices are falling, on the other personal computers have more and more memory. These facilities, currently only found on large, expensive AI workstations will become available in small, cheap shells which run on personal computers.

SUMMARY

There is a large variety of expert system shells on the market which makes the buying decision very difficult. This chapter has considered the factors to take into account when choosing a package. It started with a look at programming languages, that is, the languages used to create the shells. Whilst the end user is not going to get into the nuts and bolts of the actual program, some knowledge of languages is important. The language in which the package is written affects the way it works. The chapter continued with a review of the characteristics of expert system shells that are important: hardware, company, home or abroad, performance, registered software, help, support, existing applications and cost. At the end of the chapter is a checklist for choosing an expert system shell.

CHECKLIST FOR CHOOSING AN EXPERT SYSTEM SHELL

Company Policy

Is there a company Information System Policy?
Are there constraints on the purchase or use of hardware?
Is there existing hardware?
Will the shell run on existing hardware?
Are you expected to purchase home produced software?
Can you purchase from abroad?

Rules

How many rules can a rule set have?
How many conditions can be specified in the premise of a rule?
Is there an explanation facility for each rule?
Is there a rule dictionary?

Knowledge Acquisition

How easy is it to add, delete, modify rules?
Are there adequate text processing facilities for generating rules and explanation?
Is there a pro forma to help developers create rules?
Are rules automatically added to the rule dictionary?
Can rule sets be combined easily?
Are rule sets compiled to make execution faster?

Testing

Is there a tracing facility for developers to follow the reasoning of the inference engine step-by-step?
Can the knowledge base be partitioned to allow testing of subsets of rules?
Is there a way to automate the testing of all rules?
Can the inference engine print an interaction to allow detailed study?

Inference Engine

Can the inference engine perform forward chaining?
Can the inference engine perform backward chaining?
Can it do both?
Can it handle uncertainty? How?
Does the inference engine interface with other packages?
Can it input and output data?

Using the Shell

Does the inference work quickly?
Even with a large knowledge base?
Does the shell make full use of graphics, windows and menus?

Help

Is there onscreen help available at all times?
Is this help context sensitive?
Are manuals provided?
Are they readable? Helpful? Easy to use?

Supplier

Is the supplier also the producer?
Is the supplier well established? Respectable?
What level of support is available?
Is there hot line support?
Someone at the other end of the telephone?
Does the supplier offer training? Consultation?

The Shell

What version of the shell is currently available?
Are there existing applications you can study?
Are there example knowledge bases provided with the shell?
Will there be future upgrades?
Will your existing applications be compatible with any future upgrades?

Cost

How much does the shell cost?
What do you get for the money? Software? Manuals? Support?
What will the total system cost?

Security

Can you build in security controls?
Can you restrict access to the knowledge base?
Can you assign and update passwords?

9
Available Shells

INTRODUCTION

The following is a listing of currently available shells that are rule-based, although the larger packages are also rule inducing, see Chapter ten. Most will run on an IBM PC or compatible unless stated otherwise. In addition, there are a few much larger systems. These are included because they are in widespread use or scaled down versions are becoming available. This list, inevitably, is not fully comprehensive but it does give a reasonable guide to what is available. Prices are given for comparative purposes only. It should be bourne in mind that the larger and more expensive shells will be sold as a package which includes not only the software but also training, support, consultancy and annual maintenance fees. Specifications and prices are constantly changing, check with suppliers who are listed in Chapter twelve.

SHELLS

Name: Adviser
Supplier: ICL UK
Cost: £1500 for the mainframe version.

Although marketed in December 1984, Adviser has earlier origins being based on another shell called Sage. It runs on ICL mainframes, but it is being ported down to the ICL personal computer, the Quattro. Adviser, written in Pascal, is similar to Envisage, also adapted from Sage, which runs on a Vax mainframe computer.

Name: apes 1
Supplier: Logic Programming Associates UK
Cost: £150 + VAT

First marketed in 1984, apes (Augmented PROLOG for Expert Systems) is an expert system shell based on micro-PROLOG 3.1, which is included in the price, although each can be purchased separately. Because it is fully compatible, it gives the full range of PROLOG facilities.

Name: Chloe
Supplier: BHRA UK
Cost: £7000

Chloe is a large shell, developed in parallel with the engineering application discussed in Chapter five. It features backward and forward chaining, interfacing to external software, such as routines and procedures, and well developed explanation facilities.

Name: Crystal
Supplier: Intelligent Environments Ltd UK
Cost: £695 + VAT

Originally intending to concentrate on applications, IE Ltd have recently launched their shell as a stand alone product. Written in C, Crystal is very fast in operation and it will interface with other packages. It will handle up to 5000 rules which can be accessed via a rule dictionary.

Name: Deja Vu
Supplier: Intelligent Environments Ltd UK
Cost: £295 + VAT

From the same supplier as Crystal, Deja Vu is not a standard rule-based expert system. Rather, it is an electronic notepad which can be used for linking data to form the basis of decision modelling. This may seem difficult to get to grips with but it works well in practice.

Name: Envisage
Supplier: Systems Designers Scientific UK
Systems Designers Software Inc. USA
Cost: £10 000

Envisage is an enhanced version of Sage. Launched in December 1984, it has enhanced interfacing with other packages and a choice of man–machine interfaces. Currently, it will run only on mainframes such as a Vax.

Name: ESP Advisor
Supplier: Expert Systems International Inc. USA
Expert Systems International Ltd UK
Cost: £595 + VAT for IBM PC version

First marketed in June 1984, ESP Advisor is in widespread use. It is particularly suited to advice-giving systems, since it uses a facility called text animation which can be used to build text frames. Written in PROLOG-2, ESP Advisor can handle up to 3000 rules and interface with all PROLOG-2 facilities

Name: Expert Edge
Supplier: Helix Expert Systems Ltd UK
Cost: no longer available

Expert Edge is written in C and is based on an earlier product Tess (The Expert System Shell). It is a straightforward rule-based system that makes effective use of windows and menus to help the developer and the user. There is an inbuilt facility for giving explanation to the user.

Name: Expert Edge Advanced
Supplier: Helix Expert Systems Ltd UK
Cost: £1800 + VAT for IBM PC version

Expert Edge Advanced is an enhanced version of Expert Edge which runs faster and gives the user more control over the screen windows and format.

Name: Expert Edge Professional
Supplier: Helix Expert Systems Ltd UK
Cost: £3700 + VAT for IBM PC version

Expert Edge Professional is an enhanced version of Expert Edge Advanced. It gives improved interfaces to external programs and an interactive video disk interface, which, it is proposed, could form the basis of interactive presentations with users.

Name: FrameEngine
Supplier: Expert Systems International Inc. USA
Expert Systems International Ltd UK
Cost: £995 + VAT

FrameEngine, as the name suggests, uses frames to formalise

knowledge and rules to manipulate it. Written in PROLOG 2, like its younger sibling, ESP Advisor, FrameEngine is intended for experienced users who may want to access PROLOG facilities.

Name: Guru
Supplier: Database Experts Ltd UK
Micro Data Base Systems USA
Cost: £2995

Based on the well established Knowledgeman, Guru is an integrated package that incorporates a relational database, a spreadsheet, text processing, graphics and an expert systems shell. It does run on a personal computer but it requires a 5 megabyte hard disk. Written in C, Guru is a complex package. A demonstration version is available.

Name: Hypnotist
Supplier: Intelligence Products UK
Cost: £600

Whilst Hypnotist is a rule-based expert system, it is particularly suitable for creating control mechanisms, which may run according to pre-determined timescales. Hypnotist will collect and act upon on-line data. A demonstration version is available.

Name: Inference ART Release 2
Supplier: Ferranti Computer Systems Ltd UK
Inference Corp USA
Cost: $75 000

Inference ART is one of the big three expert system shells in the USA. Originally written in LISP for dedicated AI workstations, such as the TI Explorer, Sun and Symbolics machines, it is being rewritten to make it more widely accessible on other hardware, for example, DEC.

Name: KEE
Supplier: Artificial Intelligence Ltd UK
Intellicorp USA
Cost: £31 750 + VAT

Another of the big three US shells, KEE (Knowledge Engineering Environment), was launched in August 1983. Written in LISP, it has Prolog-style programming. KEE uses a frame-based knowledge base and has facilities for forward and backward chaining. It runs on the Xerox range of AI Workstations.

Name: KES
Supplier: Software Architecture and Engineering, Inc. USA
Software Architecture and Engineering UK
Cost: £2500 + VAT for IBM PC

KES (Knowledge Engineering System) was launched in 1983. Written in LISP, it will integrate with existing software. Rules are entered using the Parser and verified using the KES Inspector. KES will run on AI workstations and VAX mainframes.

Name: KES 2.3
Supplier: Software Architecture and Engineering, Inc. USA
Software Architecture and Engineering UK
Cost: £2500 + VAT for IBM PC

KES 2.3 is based on KES but is implemented in C, rather than LISP, because it is quicker, up to 10 times faster on an IBM PC. Also, it makes it available on a wider range of hardware systems. KES 2.3 supports two inference systems with a third, using Bayes' theorem, being added in 1987.

Name: KnowledgeCraft
Supplier: Carnegie Group Inc. USA
Carnegie (U.K.) Ltd UK
Cost: $50 000, approximately £35 000

KnowledgeCraft is the third of the US big three. Written in LISP, it will run on Symbolics and Texas Instruments AI workstations or VAX mainframes. It is intended to scale down KnowledgeCraft for personal computers to be available in 1987.

Name: Knowledgeman/2
Supplier: Database Experts Ltd UK
Cost: £595 +VAT

Knowledgeman/2, also known as Kman/2, is based on Knowledgeman. Written in C, it includes a range of facilities: data management, spreadsheet analysis and text processing, in addition to an integral expert system shell.There is also a range of add-on enhancements: K-Graph, K-Chat, K-Paint, K-Report, K-Text, K-Comm and K-Mouse.

Name: Knowol
Supplier: Intelligent Machine Company USA
Cost: $39.95

Knowol is a good example of the new breed of 'What the Heck' software. 'It is so cheap, if it is a disaster, what the ...' However, Knowol is a full expert system shell with good on-screen help and a readable manual that can handle simple rules with backward chaining.

Name: Leonardo
Supplier: Creative Logic Ltd
Cost: Level 1 £149 + VAT, 2 £695 + VAT, 3 £1995 + VAT

Leonardo is a recent addition to the range of shells available. Launched in March 1987, it is offered in three versions or levels. All three are rule-based shells with a built-in procedural language and a frame structure. Level 1 is the entry system, allowing users to develop up to 1000 lines of rule text. Level 2 has no restrictions. Level 3 is aimed at the professional knowledge engineer with facilities for Bayesian rules and fuzzy logic.

Name: M1 Version 2
Supplier: Framentec France
Teknowledge USA
Cost: $5000

Framentec is a French company, combining Teknowledge of Palo Alto and Framatome, a French multinational. M1 Version 2 is a rule-based system that can handle up to 1000 knowledge base entries at a time. It makes full use of menus, windows and colour.

Name: Micro Expert
Supplier: ISI Ltd UK
McGraw Hill Book Co. USA
Cost: £300 for IBM PC version

Micro Expert was launched in 1981. Written in Pascal, it can handle backward and forward chaining reasoning. The shell is available for a variety of hardware including the IBM, Apricot and the BBC B. It can handle up to 500 rules.

Name: MICRO-PS
Supplier: Ashton-Tate US
Cost: $29.95

MICRO-PS is a scaled down version of KES and is given with a copy of 'Building Your First Expert System', a book published by Ashton-Tate, see Chapter 13. Whilst a limited system, it is an inexpensive look at expert system shells and PROLOG-type programming.

Name: Personal Consultant
Supplier: Texas Instruments Inc. USA
Texas Instruments Ltd UK
Cost: £695 + VAT

Personal Consultant is a fully implemented expert system shell written in LISP. Originally only available to run on Texas Instruments' own hardware, the TI Professional Computer, it has been ported across to run on MSDOS systems, including the IBM PC. TI intend to produce a smaller version of Personal Consultant, called PC Easy.

Name: Personal Consultant Plus
Supplier: Texas Instruments Inc. USA
Texas Instruments Ltd UK
Cost: £1995 + VAT

Personal Consultant Plus is an enhanced version of Texas Instruments' Personal Consultant. It has a more sophisticated development module allowing for the faster development of larger systems. It also has the ability to interface with other software such as data base and graphics programs.

Name: Reveal
Supplier: ICL UK
Cost: £30 000

Reveal is a comprehensive package written in Fortran which includes a relational database. It has built-in modelling facilities for financial applications, for example, mortgages. It can handle fuzzy knowledge and outputs both reports and graphics. Reveal requires an ICL or alternative mainframe.

Name: Sage
Supplier: Systems Designers Scientific UK
Systems Designers Software Inc. USA
Cost: £1000 for IBM PC version

Sage is a mature shell, first marketed in April 1982. It is capable of handling fuzzy logic and interfacing with other packages. Written in Pascal, it will run on a range of hardware from Vax mainframes to IBM PCs and compatibles. An enhanced version, Envisage, was launched in December 1984.

Name: Savoir
Supplier: ISI Ltd UK
Cost: £3000 for IBM PC version

First marketed in September 1984, Savoir is one of the largest selling shells worldwide. Written in Pascal, it will handle up to 2250 rules when running on an MSDOS personal computer but it will run on mainframes and minis. ISI Ltd is jointly owned by ISIS Systems and ICI.

Name: XI
Supplier: Expertech Ltd UK
Cost: £595 + VAT for IBM PC version

Expertech's XI was launched in the summer of 1985 and has become widespread. Written in PROLOG-2, it is derived from Props, a system developed at the Imperial Cancer Research Fund's laboratory. XI is aimed at first-time and end users and a tutorial system is available.

Name: XI Plus
Supplier: Expertech Ltd UK
Cost: £1250 + VAT for IBM PC version

XI Plus is an enhanced version of XI intended for data processing department users. It has the facility to link to standard personal computer packages including spreadsheets, databases and graphics. It is capable of both forward and backward reasoning.

10
An Alternative Approach

INTRODUCTION

So far in this book we have considered expert systems which are a set of rules generated by an expert and put into a knowledge base. Such a knowledge base forms the basis of an application which is subsequently accessed by a user who interrogates the rules. This approach assumes that the rules can be collected together with no difficulty. However, this is not always the case. As yet the science, or perhaps art, of knowledge acquisition is in its infancy. We have not fully developed methods and techniques for putting knowledge into rules and, thus, creating a knowledge base. This inherent difficulty in putting knowledge into the system in the form of rules is known as the 'engineering bottleneck'. Inference engines, user interfaces and knowledge bases, once created, work well enough. The difficulty is creating the knowledge base. This is partly due to the way organisations and individuals actually work. Individuals within an organisation may have spent several years doing something using instinctive guidelines without necessarily formulating formal rules. Is it then always necessary to create a set of rules to capture the past experience? The answer, of course, is no. What is needed is a rule-inducing expert system.

RULE-INDUCING SYSTEMS

A rule-inducing system takes an existing body of data or past performance, such as that held in a database like dBase III, and attempts to work out if there are any inherent rules in the data which are valid and consistent. Imagine for the last few years that you have been appointing staff according to certain criteria. You know what the criteria are but you are not sure just what the internal balance and weighting is between the factors. The solution is to enter the data into a rule-inducing system. Let us assume further that there are eight factors. The first is the person's name which should not affect selection. The following seven factors are appearance, training, intellect, aptitude, interests, character and situation. Each factor is given a range of possible options, for example, appearance can be impressive, smart, casual, or untidy. Clearly the factors and options will vary with each system. Then there is an outcome for each candidate with three possibilities: accepted, rejected or possible. A complete list of factors may look like this:

appearance:
- —impressive
- —smart
- —casual
- —untidy

training:
- —senior
- —middle
- —junior

intellect:
- —good
- —medium
- —low

aptitudes:
- —mechanical
- —literacy
- —artistic
- —numeracy

interests :
- —academic
- —social
- —practical
- —artistic

character:
- —innovative
- —reliable
- —extrovert
- —introvert

situation:
- —single
- —married

selection:
- —accepted
- —possible
- —rejected

Having identified the relevant factors for applicants, we can complete a table of data giving an entry for each candidate for each factor or attribute. Such a collection of data may look like Figure 11.

Having completed a table of examples we can ask the rule-inducing package to identify any inherent rules within the factors. Putting the data in Figure 11 through SuperExpert generated these rules:

```
IF character = innovative
    AND intellect = good THEN accepted
    AND intellect = medium THEN null
    AND intellect = low THEN rejected

IF character = reliable
    AND interests = social
        AND training = senior THEN accepted
        AND training = middle THEN possible
        AND training = junior THEN null
    AND interests = academic THEN accepted
    AND interests = practical THEN rejected
    AND interests = artistic THEN possible

IF character = extrovert
    AND intellect = good THEN accepted
    AND intellect = medium THEN possible
    AND intellect = low THEN null

IF character = introvert THEN rejected
```

In this particular example we have 'null' outcomes, which means the system was unable to draw a conclusion in certain circumstances. We can see by glancing at the rules created that there has been some order in our past chaos. We always reject introverts, no matter what other characteristics they may have. If we want to simplify selection in the future using the same criteria, we do not need to investigate all factors.

	NAME	APPEARANCE	TRAINING	INTELLECT	APTITUDES	INTERESTS	CHARACTER	SITUATION	SELECTION
1	EMILY HAMNETT	smart	junior	good	mechanical	academic	innovative	married	accepted
2	ALISON HAYES	casual	middle	low	literacy	social	reliable	married	possible
3	MARY BARCLAY	untidy	junior	good	literacy	practical	extrovert	single	accepted
4	CATHERINE JONES	casual	senior	medium	artistic	artistic	introvert	single	rejected
5	MARK RANDLE	smart	junior	good	literacy	academic	reliable	married	accepted
6	NICK WADDINGTON	impressive	middle	good	artistic	social	extrovert	single	accepted
7	FIONA HOLMES	impressive	middle	medium	numeracy	practical	extrovert	single	possible
8	CLARE SURTEES	casual	junior	low	mechanical	practical	reliable	married	rejected
9	JOHN SMITH	smart	middle	low	mechanical	artistic	innovative	single	rejected
10	ADRIAN WRIGHT	untidy	junior	good	artistic	academic	introvert	single	rejected
11	SARAH JACKSON	smart	middle	good	numeracy	social	innovative	married	accepted
12	CHRIS WILLMOTT	casual	senior	medium	literacy	social	reliable	single	accepted
13	JAMES WALTERS	impressive	middle	medium	literacy	practical	introvert	single	rejected
14	JOHN BARNETT	casual	senior	good	numeracy	artistic	reliable	married	possible
15	HENRY ROBINSON	smart	middle	medium	literacy	social	reliable	single	possible
16	JANE HOWARD	casual	junior	good	artistic	academic	extrovert	single	accepted

Figure 11: *An Example Database*

We start by weeding out the introverts. A further analysis of the rules reveal that we do not use the information relating to situation, aptitudes and appearance. We may congratulate ourselves on our unbiased approach to selection. Alternatively we might ask ourselves why we collect this information in the first place.

Looking through rules generated from our own past experiences can be a rewarding exercise. We discover ourselves, or, at least, we discover how we have worked in the past, which should give some indications of how we will act in the future. However, we do not need to dig our way through the rules each time we have a new candidate. Once the rules have been created, using a rule-inducing package we can store them for future use and interrogate them whenever it is necessary. In case you are an introvert, it should be emphasised that the above data and induced rules are only examples.

INTERROGATING A RULE SET

Having created a rule set using historical data it is possible to use the rules in the same way as a rule-based system. Let us assume the above rules have been induced and you choose to interrogate. The system will ask you to choose the options for each of the factors that correspond to the current candidate, thus:

```
Select prompt letter for character:
a) innovative b) reliable c) extrovert d) introvert
```

You may feel that the person has an innovative character and so you respond 'a'. Assuming that the character is innovative, that is, choice 'a', the second layer of the rule is displayed showing the choice of intellect.

```
Select prompt letter for intellect:
a) good b) medium c) low
```

You could respond 'a' which will give

```
Answer is: accepted
```

In other words:

> if character = innovative and intellect = good
> then the candidate will be accepted

Another enquiry may follow these lines:

The screen will display:

Select prompt letter for character:
a) innovative b) reliable c) extrovert d) introvert

Then, for example, you could respond 'b'. This leads to various interests being displayed.

Select prompt letter for interests:
a) social b) academic c) practical d) artistic

Suppose you select 'a', another layer of the rule is invoked because the level of training is now relevant.

Select prompt letter for training:
a) senior b) middle c) junior

Responding 'b' will give

Answer is: possible

Here the line of reasoning followed is:

if character = reliable and interest = social
    and training = middle
        then the candidate will be possible

HOW DO RULE-INDUCING SYSTEMS WORK?

How does a rule-inducing system go from past experience to a set of rules? Firstly, the inducer must have access to information that is sufficiently structured for it to be analysed easily. We have yet to reach the stage where the system will make order from chaos. The information can be taken from a relational database such as dBase III which is highly structured.

A relational database consists of a set of records, also called relations or tuples, which contain data about particular factors or fields. In the example above, each candidate is a record and appearance, training and intellect are fields. Each record in the example above contains data but some rule-inducers will handle incomplete sets of data.

One field, that is, one piece of information for record must be the target field, for example, profit, acceptance, success, good weather, etc. Any field can be a target as long as it is dependent or is thought to be dependent on the others.

When the data has been structured into a usable form the inducer will work through the records and try to identify the rules inherent in the fields that will give the required target. There are two options here. Either the rule-inducer will work on the whole data, which is reasonable if the data base is small, or it will take some of the records, say half, and generate the rules using incomplete data. Either way it will formulate the rule for the first record and then test it against the second and so on. Eventually the rule will have been tested against all example records. As further examples are added so the inducer will test the formulated rules against them. The rules will be modified to accommodate more and more data. Eventually a clear, concise and universal set of rules will be generated which can be interrogated.

However, in some cases the inducer may not be able to generate a rule or rules because the data is contradictory. The rule-inducer will respond in various ways according to the package. The inducer could continue looping forever, unable to define a rule. It could say there is no rule system available. Alternatively, the rule-inducer may create endless rules that are circular and tautological. Another approach is to remove rules that are contradictory and put them 'on the shelf' to allow the user to decide what to do with them. Finally a rule-inducer could assign probabilities to the rules so that the rules apply some of the time, for example, 'if the person had brown hair then you appointed x% of the time in the past'. Such an approach perhaps best reflects the way we work in practice based on the simplest logic: 'this is what we tended to do in the past'.

Having created the rules, these can be listed and used in future analysis, in effect the user now has a rule-based system. Some packages allow the transfer of rules into a higher level language such as C or Pascal so that a program written in that language can run on a computer using the rules created.

AREAS OF APPLICATION

Once a rule-inducing package has induced the rules from a database, they can be used in the same way as a rule-based expert system. The final outcome of either approach is very similar, a system that will give advice to non-experts. However, they do have different starting points.

A rule-based system will require an expert or experts whose knowledge can be translated into and stored as a set of rules. Conversely a rule-inducing system requires data that will yield a rule structure. Thus any area that is going to be used to form the basis of a rule-induced system must have certain characteristics. The data must have a set of clearly defined attributes.

In the example quoted at the beginning of this chapter these were appearance, training, intellect, etc. The data must include a set of defined values such as high, medium, low, etc. These values should be based on relevant examples. Finally, there must be some causality within the data. In other words, there should be no random or stochastic influences. In the case of the selection example the final outcome, accepted, possible or rejected, should be based on the attributes listed. It is possible to have a relational database with clearly defined attributes or fields and lots of examples or records but which does not have any inherent causality. I have a database of my small wine cellar. Would it help me to induce rules from this database which can only inform me: if the wine is Bordeaux it is from France and if the wine is Valpolicella it is from Italy? Clearly, such a database will not give a reasonable set of rules. The following are just some of the areas where a useful set of rules could be induced:

PERSONNEL

The selection example given at the beginning of this chapter was for illustrative purposes only. Any personnel specialist would be concerned if such a system were used in practice. Nonetheless, the idea is sound. All organisations occasionally have to recruit staff. Most organisations have some form of selection procedure which will involve matching potential candidates against selected criteria. Such comparisons can be used to generate a database which subsequently can be used to generate the rules used in selection. There may be some benefit in making explicit the assumptions, that is, informal rules, used in past selection. It may be easier to use past experience to create the rules than trying to write the rules themselves. The selection of candidates is done not just for a job but also for promotion or training. Any selection procedure could use the format of the example above.

FAULT FINDING

When a system fails then it fails in a particular way and with a certain set of characteristics. If these characteristics are known then a rule-inducing system can be used to identify links of causality. An example may be a car that fails to function properly. We can clearly identify the fault, for example, pinking, and we can note the current characteristics of the car, for example, timing setting, carbon monoxide emission, air/petrol ratio. The system will tell us that pinking occurs when a particular set of conditions occur. Similarly, such a system could be used to identify the reasons for rejects in a production system, failures in process production or breakdowns in batch processing.

MARKETING

If we are responsible for the marketing aspects of an organisation, we should know how much we are spending, what we are actually doing and how we are performing in the various markets. If we can identify the factors in each market that lead to successful sales, we can create a database of these factors which we can pass through a rule-inducing system. This should create a rule set telling us what combination of things in each market is giving us success or failure. Then, we can make judgements about marketing strategy in all our markets that will bring the best rewards for us.

BRANCHES

Just as we may operate in several markets, our organisation may function as separate branches or outlets, for example franchises. What is it about a particular branch that makes it more successful than another? If we can identify what we consider to be the relevant factors we can piece the jigsaw together. The factors may include capital investment, location, stock levels, personality of the manager and local employment levels. As long as we can identify the factors, the rule-inducer will make the links by inducing the relevant rules and so help us make all our branches successful.

STOCK

During periods of economic expansion we can afford to carry large stocks of raw materials, consumables, whatever. Indeed, such stocks are a necessary part of growth. However, during periods of economic uncertainty or contraction we become very concerned about tying up large amounts of cash in stock. Currently, our concern is reflected in the popularity of such notions as minimum stock levels, JIT (Just In Time) manufacturing, minimum order quantities, etc. Rule-inducing systems can contribute to good stock control. All stock items have characteristics, for example, shelf life, bulk, cost, minimum stock level, minimum reorder period, etc. These factors can be entered into a rule-inducing expert system to establish good stock control by determining when and how much stock should be re-ordered.

The examples given above indicate some of the scope for rule-inducing systems. We can induce useful rules in a variety of situations, provided there is a structured database, enough examples and some inherent causality within the data.

ADVANTAGES

Whilst any organisation will conduct its affairs according to guidelines laid down within the organisation or imposed from outside, it is unlikely that these guidelines are clearly stated anywhere in the organisation. Furthermore, it is unlikely that they are explicit, written down or always strictly adhered to by all employees. Rather, employees use rule of thumb roughly within corporate guidelines to manage their day-to-day affairs. Such rule of thumb leads to an accumulation of experience within the organisation kept as a collection of data rather than a set of rules. Clearly, it could be advantageous to create an explicit set of rules. Rather than use a knowledge base engineer to analyse a situation and then draw up rules why not use a rule-inducing package to run through the data and establish any inherent rules?

Not only will an organisation have masses of data requiring analysis and understanding but also it is likely that such information will be held on a computer. This will be true for payrolls, possibly for invoices, some will have extensive systems covering customers, markets, stock, etc. This data will form the basis of a rule-induced system and can be read directly into the computer by the software without the need to retype or interpret the data at all.

One difficulty with creating rules is the need to determine not only conditions but outcomes. We must decide for all possibilities what the outcome will be. A rule-inducing system uses the experiences of past outcomes rather than creating them. It relates to the real world with real data rather than dealing in abstract concepts like rules.

DISADVANTAGES

Although there are benefits in letting the system define the rules for you, there are inevitably problems with such an approach. Rule-inducing systems do have inbuilt problems:

EARLY VERSIONS

All of AI can be said to be in its infancy. Although rule-inducers have been available for some years, it is only recently that they are starting to be sold as stand alone application packages and not just esoteric research tools. In consequence, they tend to be spartan and unfriendly compared with their close relatives, the rule-based systems.

WIDE OPEN SPACES

Creating a set of rules allows the opportunity to cover areas even if there is no past experience but the induction of rules from existing data is more stringent. Clearly the data must be available if the inducer is going to create a complete and useful set of rules. This will not always be the case. For a variety of reasons, such as bad book-keeping, modesty or belligerence you may not have complete data for all cases or examples. How will the rule-inducer cope with these omissions? Either it will disregard the gaps and induce rules from existing data or it will assume default values which will give more data but may lead to inaccuracy in the final rules. Either way it should explain what it is doing.

AS A RULE

If you are creating your own rules then the content and meaning ought to be clear to the user. This is not quite so apparent when the rules are induced by the computer. A few examples will illustrate the pitfalls that may occur. Suppose you set up the personnel system given as an example previously in this chapter. Furthermore, you want to establish causality, that is to say, identify what causes what. Inducing the rules will give the basis for previous applicants being accepted, rejected or considered as possibles. This assumes that the characteristics are the basis of selection, but the reverse may be true.

Let us revise the request and ask the system to induce the basis for the characteristics. Now we discover, say, that all accepted people have blue eyes rather than all blue-eyed people are accepted. There is a problem of causality. Do we appoint because of blue eyes or do they have blue eyes because they are appointed. It may seem obvious in this example which way round we are working, but it is less clear in other situations, for example, are we promoted because we attend courses or do we attend courses because we are promoted? Allowing others to create our rules can lead to confusion.

Even apparently simple situations can be rather complex. Suppose one of our factors for recruitment is age. We may have the following examples as a basis for rule-induction:

Example	Name	Age	Outcome
1	Smith	18	Reject
2	Brown	25	Accept
3	Green	33	Accept
4	Jones	30	Accept
5	Davies	17	Reject

It is fairly evident from this data that age has some bearing on acceptance or rejection. The two younger people are rejected and the elder three are accepted. So far so good, but what is the rule to be induced? We can say with some certainty:

If age <= (is equal to or less than) 18
Then reject

If age => (is equal to or greater than) 25
Then accept

What happens if the next candidate is 19 years of age? A rule inducing system can do one of several things. It can evaluate that the value lies between two defined points and use the nearest point upwards, in other words 19 is greater than 18 and the next age up is 25 and the person is accepted. Similarly, it can say that 19 is less than 25 and look for the next point down which is 18 and say the person is rejected. A little more sophisticated but equally unreliable is to take an average of the available examples and extrapolate from it. Thus the average of 18 and 25 is 21.5, anyone over this age will be accepted and anyone below will be rejected. However, 20 may be the actual cut off point and we may wish to exclude all persons who are 20 and younger. To do this we can either stipulate that 21 is a cut off point and the system should reject all who do not qualify or we enter two contrived examples, thus:

Example	Name	Age	Outcome
6	Aardvark	20	Reject
7	Zoe	21	Accept

The rule-inducer will consider the two examples and determine that there is one rule applying

If age > 20
  Then accept

However, to tidy up the situation we have been forced to create rules either by setting conditions or by deliberately creating false examples to create limits. Either way the rule-inducer has required help and is not solving all our problems. The difficulties encountered with age will occur when a factor can have various possible attributes and not all of these occur naturally in the examples, particularly numerical values. As an example we saw in our data base that one factor was Training with the possible attributes of Junior, Middle and Senior. Suppose we now have a candidate with no training at all. Will this person be accepted, rejected or will the rules developed from our data base refuse to give an answer until we choose one of the three current options. Different rule-inducing shells approach the problem differently.

CONSISTENCY

We can tell by inspecting the rules generated at the beginning of this chapter that they make sense. To remind you, the rules were:

```
IF character = innovative
    AND intellect = good THEN accepted
    AND intellect = medium THEN null
    AND intellect = low THEN rejected
IF character = reliable
    AND interests = social
        AND training = senior THEN accepted
        AND training = middle THEN possible
        AND training = junior THEN null
    AND interests = academic THEN accepted
    AND interests = practical THEN rejected
    AND interests = artistic THEN possible
IF character = extrovert
    AND intellect = good THEN accepted
    AND intellect = medium THEN possible
    AND intellect = low THEN null
```

IF character = introvert THEN rejected

We could go through all the examples and check that the rules work in each case. Taking the first example as a test case, we find for Emily Hamnett that character = innovative, intellect = good and selection = accepted. Checking all sixteen examples we would find that the rules hold true for all of them. However, this may be a reasonably simple exercise for the size of database and rules we have in this example. It is not feasible to carry out a similar exercise for large scale applications. We would have to rely on the rules generated, although we could test the rules against a sample of examples. Whilst the rule may be valid it may not be consistent. Using the same data we may be able to create a different set of rules. It is possible that there is a very simple rule governing the data which has not been generated, for example, we only appoint married extroverts. A different package may give us an equally valid but different rule set.

When we add another example to a database we may wish to re-create the rules. This additional example may require a completely new set of rules that look nothing like the original set and which use attributes previously not considered. This does not mean that the new rule set is invalid, it merely highlights the lack of control that the user has over the way rules are induced. Any rule set generated using a tried and tested, reputable rule-inducing package will be valid based on the examples used. The question remains, are the examples enough to clearly define a useful and reliable rule set?

DEVELOPING RULE-INDUCED SYSTEMS

In the preceding chapters we have seen that rule-based systems are attempts at embodying knowledge from an expert, in a computer to be used subsequently by users who are non-experts. Essentially, rule-inducing systems are the same, they attempt to create a knowledge base from existing data to be used by non-experts. The difference lies in the way the knowledge is created, either it is entered as a set of rules or it is induced from existing data. The outcome is much the same except for some differences that are worth considering.

BUILDING

A rule-based system will involve a group of people including the expert or experts, a knowledge base engineer and possibly a knowledge base administrator. These roles will be slightly different in a rule-inducing system. The expert is no longer a person or persons but a collection of data in a database. To extract the rules requires the skills of someone familiar with the rule-inducing shell. This person may not be a knowledge engineer in the same sense as a KBE with rule-based systems. To create a system requires a series of different stages with different skills required. Firstly, the relevant factors must be determined. Secondly, examples must be found and catalogued to create sufficient data for the inducer to work. Finally, the rules will be induced from the available data. Of course, it is possible to use an existing database and create rules fairly easily but in new applications the development of factors and examples can be a difficult problem.

Similarly, the knowledge base will have to be administered, maintained, kept up to date, and expanded, all tasks of the knowledge base administrator but a different KBA to one maintaining a rule-based system. The tasks, whilst having the same names, are slightly different.

UPDATING

There are a variety of reasons why a system may need to be updated. Any system as stated earlier is locked into a point of time and reflects the levels of knowledge and experience of that age. Similarly, a rule-inducing system is based on current not future examples. We may want to modify the rules to incorporate changes in the examples. This can be achieved by accessing particular examples using search techniques within database software. We may want to update the data for all introverts. The command would be:

```
find examples for character = introvert
        and replace selection with accepted
```

Alternatively, additional examples can be added to the database. As examples are added, the rule inducer can either check existing rules to ensure they are still valid or induce new rules to accommodate any changes.

Most rule-inducing systems allow for the generated rules to be incorporated into programming languages, such as Pascal, and the additional knowledge can be added to the program. Since the developers of rule-inducing systems have concentrated on the software required to generate rules they have spent less time on user friendliness and accessing rules. It is assumed that the inducer creates the rules which are subsequently used by the user who will never see the examples or the actual rules. In consequence the editing facilities are geared toward computer experts and not end-users.

HELP

Similarly, the level of help available with rule-inducing systems is generally sparse. The shells are written for computer experts often based on research models that have been packaged for sale to the 'public'. Having dug around inside the organisation to create the factors, then the examples and finally the rules, the user is faced with a series of short and unfriendly questions based on the rules. Because the computer is generating the rules simply on the basis of causality, in other words, what goes with what to give what, it cares little for help to the user. Asking the question 'why?' will elicit no response from from a rules-inducing system.

The more sophisticated the package, the more it will combine features of rule-based and rule-inducing systems, with the ability to use data to create rules which can then be modified, entered into a dictionary and help added in the same way as rule-based systems allow. As systems develop, so the good points of both approaches are incorporated into shells that are friendlier, quicker and more powerful in the things they can do.

AVAILABLE SYSTEMS

Whilst there is a fair range of rule-inducing systems, the choice is more limited than rule-based systems currently available. The following packages represent a range available 'across the counter', that is, they can be purchased and run by any user with the appropriate hardware. The factors influencing the choice of a rule-inducing package should reflect the factors discussed in relation to rule-based systems, with the caveat that rule-inducing systems are more for the expert computer user and tend to be more austere in their packaging and help. Costs are given for comparison purposes. All software producers and sellers will respond to market trends and economies of scale and so prices will fall according to the success or otherwise of the products. Some of the large shells mentioned in chapter nine also have a rule-inducing module.

Name: ACLS
Supplier: Southdata Ltd UK
Cost: £875 + VAT

Analogue Computer Learning System (ACLS) is also marketed as Expert-Ease, see below. Whilst it will access data specifically created for the analysis, Southdata have enhanced ACLS to create Superfile ACLS which will read in files from Superfile, a database package also produced by them.

Name: BEAGLE
Supplier: Warm Boot Ltd UK
Cost: £100 + VAT for IBM PC version

Bionic Evolutionary Algorithm Generating Logical Expressions (BEAGLE) is a collection of modules with names such as SEED—Selectively Extracts Example Data, HERB—Heuristic Evolutionary Rule Breeder and PLUM—Procedural Language Utility Maker. Others are ROOT, STEM and LEAF. These modules combine to analyse sets of data and create rules which are ordered and then tested until the best rules are found. These can be written into Pascal and Fortran with the option of BASIC and C. It can handle 32 000 examples each with up to 64 fields. This is budget price software with manual and onscreen help to match. Future versions will no doubt be better documented.

Name: Expert-Ease
Supplier: Intelligent Terminals Ltd UK
Cost: £495 + VAT

Expert-Ease is one of the earliest rule-inducing systems. It was developed in the UK by Professor Donald Michie and his team at the Turing Institute in Glasgow. It is a well established package with good documetation and good on-screen help. Written in Pascal, Expert-Ease will produce rules in Pascal format. It is also marketed by Southdata as ACLS.

Name: ExTran 7.2
Supplier: Intelligent Terminals Ltd UK
Cost: £1995 + VAT

ExTran, now at version 7.2, is a powerful package that will induce rules from examples and also accept rules entered interactively. Written in Fortran, ExTran 7.2 will generate rules in Fortran code for interrogation by non-expert users. Further, these rules can be linked together in various formats. It consists of two parts: ACL-Tran (Analog Concept Learning Translator), not dissimilar to ACLS, which determines the rules and the Driver which runs the rules.

Name: I-1
Supplier: PAL Software UK
Cost: £750 + VAT

Intelligence-1 (I-1) handles problems within topics. A topic is the total data base and a problem is those factors chosen for their relevance to the desired outcome. Such a topic can handle up to 50 factors and a problem can relate to 18 of these. Any number of examples can be handled but the rule induction is carried out on the first 100 examples in the database. A training version of I-1 is available that gives on-screen help and a range of example applications. It costs £49.95

Name: RuleMaster
Supplier: Radian Corporation USA
Cost: $1295

Rule Master is written in C and will run on DOS, Unix and Vax systems. It will automatically generate rules from examples and produce these rules in C code for use in other applications, such as database systems. It has the facility to real-time and intermittent instrumentation data and can be used, therefore, for on-line control and fault diagnosis. RuleMaster was co-developed by Radian and Professor Donald Michie and Intelligent Terminals Limited.

Name: SuperExpert
Supplier: Intelligent Terminals Ltd UK
Cost: £695 + VAT

SuperExpert also developed by Professor Michie and his team at the Turing Institute is a manageable, friendly package. Written in Forth, it is based loosely on a spreadsheet format so anybody familiar with the layout should not experience difficulties using this package. It will read in data from other sources and will write the results into other standard commercial packages. Also available is a demonstration disk which allows a prospective user to look at example systems and also create their own.

SUMMARY

Expert systems are an attempt at encapsulating knowledge. Whilst we cannot replicate the human brain we can use a computer to store rules and interrogate these rules whenever we want. However, not all knowledge is so readily accessible. We may have the data but not necessarily any notion of the underlying rules. The answer is to use a rule-inducing system to establish the rules which can then be interrogated in the same way. This chapter considered rule-inducing expert systems. It started with a look at how they work, followed by a consideration of their strengths and weaknesses. Possible areas of application were considered and, finally, currently available shells were described briefly.

11
Getting Started

THE NEXT STEP

Having read this far you may feel that you want to go further in the world of AI and expert systems. What should you do next? The idea of creating your first expert system application may appear a daunting prospect. The very name 'expert system' is used by shell suppliers to invoke feelings of awe. Perhaps it would be less daunting if expert systems were known as 'advice givers', 'advice generators' or 'information processors'. However, the term expert system has gained fairly universal acceptance, if not approval, and so that is what you must consider building. Fortunately, a range of opportunities are available to you to go further down the path of expert systems.

BUY A SHELL

If you feel that there are possible areas of application in your business environment and you want to exploit the software the obvious step is to buy a software package, that is, a shell, and start developing a system. If you have spent a lot of time developing large computer-based systems, or you have an excellent computer department with the time and resources to help you, or you are very lucky, then go ahead. If you are none of these three, then you need to move slightly more cautiously, not so slowly that the impetus is lost and enthusiasm wanes but slowly enough to evaluate shells and applications rigourously, using the guidelines given in Chapter eight. In addition there are several other avenues available to you. Most, if not all, expert system shells are provided with example applications. The examples are generally small scale but like the above applications they will give you a feel for the way the shell works.

BUY AN APPLICATION

Rather than buying a shell and attempting to create your own system why not start by buying a system. If you can, you should choose a system, that is, a ready made application, using the shell that you will probably buy. Use it a few times to get a feel for what expert systems are, how they work in practice and what they can do for you. There are several applications readily available which are reasonably priced, certainly compared with the cost of a complete system. Expertech offer three expert systems: Expert Tutor, Statutory Sick Pay and Employment. Rather cheaper are three systems offered by Intelligent Environment: Company Car Tax, Statutory Sick Pay and Loans to Directors. Buying an application will show you what expert systems can do.

GO TO A DEMONSTRATION/CONFERENCE

Most, if not all, software houses realise that they are not selling candy floss but are in a more sophisticated selling environment which requires them to provide both information about their products and support for the users. Suppliers of expert systems will arrange demonstrations of their products in a number of ways. They demonstrate at professional exhibitions and conferences such as the Computers in Personnel Exhibition and Conference and at specialised conferences, such as the Annual Expert Systems Conference. Alternatively they will demonstrate their products on their own premises for a variety of potential customers. Finally if you have buying 'clout' they will come and demonstrate their product in your organisation.

USE PACKAGE ON TRIAL

Demonstrations show the facilities of packages in the best light, they do not always show the package 'warts and all'. Sometimes it is better to play with the package yourself for a day or two. Reputable suppliers will provide a copy to potential users for evaluation. If you do borrow a copy for a week or even a month ensure that all interested parties have an opportunity to look at it. The comments of other potential users are invaluable.

TRIAL SIZE PACKAGES

Several suppliers are rightly concerned about giving out copies of their software for evaluation. Firstly, there are problems of copying and copyright. Software houses who are anxious to recoup development costs may 'be reluctant to circulate copies that may be pirated. Secondly, and perhaps more importantly, they are concerned that the inexperienced user may be confused by the package and put off unnecessarily by the apparent complexity. It is likely that this is the potential users' first look at a different approach to computer applications. In consequence some of the producers have made smaller versions of their packages for trial purposes. Often they have all the facilities of the full size package without the facility to save your own efforts. They may come with examples that you can run, edit and generally play around with. The best trial or demo packages are free. Some you have to pay for, costs ranging from £10 to £50. They are good fun!

CHEAP SYSTEMS

Another alternative is to start with a small cheap system and then graduate to the real thing. This has an advantage of low outlay with the opportunity to try various packages. On the other hand, there are problems. Firstly, the cheaper the package the less powerful it will be generally and so will not give a good indication of subsequent usefulness of a larger expert system. Similarly, the cheaper the package the less help will be available and so the potential user may feel that packages are complex and unassailable. Finally, starting an application in one system to get a feel for it and then transferring to a bigger system is time consuming and prone to errors. Even so, the small packages are reasonable and one way to start.

GO ON A COURSE

Several organisations offer courses in developing and using expert systems. They tend to be expensive compared with some of the other options above and sometimes courses revolve around one package. It may be better initially to go to one of the free seminars offered by a supplier, which is a lengthy demonstration in disguise.

WATCH A FILM

As expert systems grow as an area of application so the related teaching material will grow and improve. There are some excellent films available on video about expert systems which graphically illustrate their potential. They are worth looking at and some are listed in Chapter thirteen.

READ

Besides books on expert systems, what they are and what they will do, there is a variety of literature of help to the potential user and some are listed in the bibliography. The variety includes journals related specifically to expert systems, the computer press which has items on expert systems, and the professional press, relating to your specific area, which will carry more and more about computing and expert systems.

ALVEY STARTER PACK

The Alvey Directorate was set up by the British government to act as a catalyst to the development of fifth generation computer systems in response to the Japanese announcement that they were moving into the fifth generation of computers. Similarly, the Microelectronics & Computer Technology Corporation was set up in the US and the EEC responded by setting up Esprit. Alvey is responsibile for bringing together academics and industrialists to concentrate on particular areas of interest, for example, the man–machine interface. One outcome of Alvey is a video, given in the bibloiography. Another is the Expert System Starter Pack, which consists of four systems, covering a range of approaches: Expert Ease, a rule-inducing forward chaining shell, ESP-Advisor, a forward chaining text animation system, MicroExpert, a backward chaining rule-based system and MicroSYNICS, a dialogue generator for creating the front ends of BASIC programs. The Starter Pack is available from the NCC.

ALVEY CLUBS

The Alvey Directorate is divided into specific areas of activity, VLSI (very large scale integration) technology, CAD (computer aided design), software engineering, IKBS (intelligent knowledge based systems), MMI (man-machine interface), systems architecture, large scale demonstrators, infrastructure and communications. One of the largest areas of activity in terms of money spent and number of firms participating and, of course, the one of direct importance to expert systems is the IKBS group. The 1986 Alvey Programme Annual Report cites the approval of 88 projects in this area, with 50 companies in consortia. Also taking part are 30 universities, three polytechnics and four research institutes. The research is organised within the framework of five Research Clubs:

—Knowledge Based Systems
—Logic Programming
—Systems Architecture
—Speech and Natural Language (jointly with MMI)
—Vision (jointly with MMI)

The Knowledge Based Systems Research Club represents the user end of systems, with projects in expert systems, intelligent front ends and intelligent computer-aided instruction.

The club's objectives are:

1 To promote the development of common tools, techniques and infrastructure.

2 To exchange research experience and results to the mutual benefits of its members.

3 To reduce the duplication of research effort and stimulate new research.

4 To present and discuss, within the club, the aims and achievements of research within the projects.

5 To exchange information concerning research and development external to Alvey (having due regard to Intellectual Property Rights).

6 To coordinate visits, organise reports, etc., for the benefit of club members.

7 To promote liaison with other Alvey clubs and with ESPRIT and other relevant European bodies.

The Club has three currently active Special Interest Groups (SIGs): Planning, Deep Knowledge and Intelligent Interfaces.

In addition to the Research Clubs, there are Alvey Expert Systems Awareness Clubs. Nine clubs have been founded, each mounting expert system development projects relevant to its own area of interest. Each club has approximately twenty members with each contributing about £10 000. Combined with university facilities, each club has the opportunity to build an expert system of significant size. The clubs, and an indication of their projects and progress to date, are given below:

(i) Finance—ALFEX

1 Evaluation of commercially available shells.

2 Investigation of non-shell implementation approaches.

3 Development of a market assessor.

4 Development of a full company health adviser.

Three of the four phases have been concluded, including a market assessor developed in PROLOG. The final system should comprise four assessors: financial health, market, context and financial sources availability. A further phase will address the market part of the system for the high-tech retail sector. The final phase will produce the full company health adviser.

(ii) Insurance—ARIES

1 Give members useful experience in developing expert systems for the insurance industry.

2 Two projects
 —clothing trade fire risk assessment.
 —buy/sell decision evaluation in equity investment.

The fire risk system has been demonstrated. The system for buy/sell evaluation is currently being developed. The ARIES Club has produced several detailed project reports.

(iii) Data Processing—DAPES

1 To transfer experience in building of expert systems from the specialist contributors (Expertech and National Computing Centre) to the club as a whole.

2 To build a significant expert system of practical use to club members.

3 Two prototypes
—a 'help desk assistant' which diagnoses users problems hosted by W. H. Smith.
—a diagnostic system for communications and equipment and user work stations hosted by the TSB.

The help desk prototype has been completed. The diagnostic protoytype is being developed. It is intended that one or both of the prototypes will be developed into a significant system.

(iv) Econometric Modelling—EMEX

1 Promote awareness of club members.

2 Develop an expert system to assist in the task of building econometric models.

A prototypic shell has been developed for use in testing the knowledge. A textual form of the knowledge has been produced and most recently the shell and the knowledge have been combined to provide feedback to the experts and so stimulate refinement of that knowledge.

(v) Project Planning—PLANIT

1 To develop a prototype interactive planning assistant (IPA) which would help planners to: react to changing circumstances while planning was being executed; react to the addition of new goals or constraints; give advice on the consequences of change; explain the functions of the plan.

2 To test the software using real test cases based on members' own data.

3 To determine the potential and the limitations of knowledge-based systems in the field of planning.

4 To identify the relevant current issues.

Three demonstrators have been constructed, one for each of the planning topics. A high level specification of IPA functionality has been completed. Progress has been made in identifying the knowledge used in planning, the structure of the knowledge and the degree of common representation which can be used across the planning topic.

(vi) Quantity Surveying—QSES

To promote the development and use of expert systems in the quantity surveying profession by exploring areas of possible application and preparing appropriate computer software.

Four extensive reports have been produced. Two expert systems are operational at the demonstration level. The next stage will continue the 'lead consultant' role to include debriefing the client, time forecasting and the integration and extension of the systems developed so far.

(vii) Real Time—RESCU

1 To increase awareness of the potential of expert system technology in the field of process engineering.
2 To make members more familiar with both technical and managerial aspects of the development of expert systems.
3 To demonstrate a real expert system application that is of close relevance to the area of interest of the club membership.

An Expert System has been installed at the ICI plant at Wilton, which gives advice to plant operators to assist them in recipe formulation and control of batch products. Consideration is being given to the specification and production of a real time Expert System shell for general application.

(viii) Transport and Travel—TRACE

1 To gain an understanding of the benefits offered by applying expert systems technology to problems in the transport and travel industries.
2 To develop a microbased system which will assist enquiry clerks in route selection and retail travel sales staff in selection of packaged holidays.

The project is advancing to prototype stage and from this the final product will be defined. Communication with remote databases, which is a key feature of this project, is being done using various participants' databases and communication networks.

(ix) Water Industry—WIESC

1 To increase awareness of the potential of expert systems technology in the water industry.

2 To build two expert systems for the industry, one for water distribution network control, and the other for sewerage rehabilitation planning. These topics cover a major part of the activities within the industry.

3 To make members more familiar with both technical and managerial aspects of the development of expert systems.

Requirement specifications have been produced for the two systems and design work is in progress. Three working groups have been set up to disseminate information to the membership. It is intended that an initial prototype is to be produced which, followed by a design revision, will lead to the development of the final prototype.

The above clubs are well established with the members contributing time, money and effort but reaping rewards. All the clubs have produced reports of their activities. Some of the clubs have produced specifications for expert systems, whilst others have working prototypes or demonstration versions. Most of the clubs are 'full', that is, they do not need further contributors to existing developments. However, it is worthwhile following the progress of an Alvey club in your functional area. In addition, there is scope for other groupings to get together and create industry knowledge bases and expert systems relevant to their particular needs.

THE FUTURE

We are currently enjoying the benefits of the fourth generation of computers. Using VLSI or very large scale integrated circuits, these computers are available cheaply and easily. They sit on the managers' desks and perform a range of activities. Starting with number crunching in the form of spreadsheets, users moved on to text processing and, then, information handling in the form of data bases. However, the original view of computer dreamers has not been lost. It was thought that computers would one day replace human beings or rather would do the things that humans do, both the physical tasks such as producing, cleaning and maintaining and also the mental tasks of problem solving and decision making. Such computers are not yet available. Certainly there are robots which will perform tasks endlessly and without error, however, such tasks are largely repetitive. Similarly, computers will perform intellectual tasks also of a repetitive nature, such as evaluating pay, printing invoices or checking stock levels. The search continues for more sophisticated systems.

Expert systems are one step in the development of artificial intelligence. At the moment we have general shells which can be used to generate particular applications. This approach has shown signs of success and expert systems applications are becoming widespread. As time goes on so these shells will become more powerful, able to handle thousands and thousands of rules very quickly. Computers will have massive amounts of memory to store these rules but also to store very sophisticated help systems. Shells will become conglomerates of the existing systems so they will be both forward and backward chaining, both rule-inducing and rule-based, and will handle masses of associated text for training systems. Also in the process of development is better means of creating and storing images and pictures. The developments in graphics using interactive laser videos and other devices will combine with expert systems to provide fully interactive, rule driven packages to be used for product knowledge, training and development and information retrieval. Just as expert systems have improved considerably over the last few years so they will improve in the future.

However, these changes are merely developments on what is and not what may be. Certainly the existing approach to expert systems should be developed, but that does not preclude the need for other developments. The development of the fifth generation of computers, largely by the Japanese, will open the door to a different order of computing. What is over the horizon? Firstly, the Japanese say the language of the next generation of computers is PROLOG. Eventually it may be another language but the suggestion it is PROLOG (an assertional language) reflects where we are going. The fifth generation is about computers handling knowledge not data.It is about computers handling ideas and solving problems not number crunching. Several ideas will come to fruition. We should see comprehensive voice and image recognition with voice and image production. Also we will see the advent of true parallel processing where the computer is able to do several things at once. This will open the door to another era with computers able to handle enormous amounts of information, making logical and perhaps illogical connections and so solve problems in the same way as the human brain.

However, the introduction of a new generation of computers will not stop the development of existing systems. There are still ten year old mainframe computers in service and producing the goods. Similarly, the personal computer of today will not become redundant overnight. In order to run AI applications it is possible to buy a chip that has LISP or PROLOG on it and install the chip in a personal computer. Whilst the machine is outwardly unchanged it will function as an AI workstation. As the technology improves so the power of the chips improve until a personal computer costing £1000, say, has the processing power of an AI workstation costing £5000. What we have is the combined availability of personal computers with the facilities of more specialised machines. The next generation of computers will be a leap forward but the existing technology still has untapped potential.

Just as we have generations of computers, so we will see generations of software. The first generation of expert systems were spartan research prototypes for use only by boffins. We have already moved into a second generation of expert systems. Now we have shells that can be used for developing real applications. The next generation of expert systems will be bigger, cheaper and faster.

One word of caution. We are unlikely to see a computer with the power of the human brain until the next century, although the hardest thing to predict is the future and it may happen sooner. Who, twenty years ago, would have predicted the personal computer in its present form? Meanwhile, we have to have reasonably priced, powerful computers that are capable of running packages that can contribute to the business environment. One such package is an expert system shell and we should learn to capatilise on the technology as much as possible.

SUMMARY

Choosing a software package to perform a familiar task such as invoicing or word processing is a difficult enough process. To choose a software package to perform tasks that are alien to the potential user is even more difficult. Whilst we make decisions based on rules or heuristics, we rarely formalise these. To create a knowledge base and thus an application we must buy a package eventually. However, there are intermediate stages. This chapter considered the things that managers can do to improve their knowledge of expert systems and applications prior to setting up their own examples. Looking beyond existing systems this chapter concluded with a brief glimpse of the future.

12
Suppliers

The following is a list of suppliers of the shells and applications mentioned previously in this book. The inclusion of a supplier is not a guaranty of their product. Readers are advised to take particular note of the hints on choosing shells given in Chapter eight. Every effort has been made to make this list fully comprehensive. However, the number of expert systems is growing daily, with the number of suppliers also increasing.

Company
Address
Telephone Number
Products

Artificial Intelligence Limited
Intelligence House
Merton Road
Watford
Herts
WD1 7BY
0923-47707
KEE

Ashton–Tate Publishing Group
10150 West Jefferson Boulevard
Culver City
California 90230
MICRO-PS

BHRA The Fluid Engineering Centre
Cranfield
Bedford
MK43 0AJ
0234-750422
Chloe

Carnegie Group Inc.
650 Commerce Court
Station Square
Pittsburgh
Pennsylvania 15219
412-642-6900
KnowledgeCraft

Carnegie (U.K.) Limited
GSI House
Stanhope Road
Camberley
Surrey
GU15 3PS
0276-26932
KnowledgeCraft

Creative Logic Limited
Brunel Science Park
Kingston Lane
Uxbridge
Middlesex
UB8 3PQ
0895-74468
Leonardo

Database Experts Limited
1 Thames Avenue
Windsor
Berkshire
SL4 1QP
0753-840197
Guru, Knowledgeman/2

Expertech Limited
172 Bath Road
Slough
SL1 3XE
0753-821321
XI, XI Plus

Expert Systems International Inc.
1700 Walnut Street
Philadelphia
Pennsylvania 19103
215-735-8510
ESP Advisor, Frame Engine

Expert Systems International Limited
9 West Way
Oxford
OX2 0JB
0865-242206
ESP Advisor, Frame Engine

Ferranti Computer Systems Limited
Tŷ Coch Way
Cwmbrân
Gwent
NP44 7XX
06333-71111
Inference Art Release 2

Framentec
La Boursidiere
R.N. 186
92350 Le Plessis-Robinson
46-30-24-74
M1 Version 2

Helix Expert Systems Limited
St. Bartholomew House
92 Fleet Street
London
EC4Y 1DH
01-583-9391
Expert Edge Advanced, Expert Edge Professional

ICL
Arndale House
Arndale Centre
Manchester
M4 3AR
061-833-9111
Adviser, Reveal

Inference Corporation
5300 W. Century Boulevard
7th. Floor
Los Angeles
California 90045
213-417-7997
Inference ART Release 2

Intellicorp
Knowledge Systems Division
1975 El Camino Real West
Mountain View
California 94040
415-965-5500
KEE

Intelligence Products
68 Babington Road
Streatham
London SW 16
01-677-7583
Hypnotist

Intelligent Environments Limited
Northumberland House
15–19 Petersham Road
Richmond
Surrey
TW10 6TP
Crystal, Deja Vu

Intelligent Terminals Limited
George House
36 North Hanover Street
Glasgow
041-552-1353
Expert-Ease, Extran 7, SuperExpert

Intelligent Machine Company
1907 Red Oak Circle
New Port Richey
Florida 33533
813-844-3262
Knowol

ISI Limited
11 Oakdene Street
Redhill
Surrey
RH1 6BT
0737-71327
Micro Expert, Savoir

Logic Programming Associates
Studio 4
The Royal Victoria Patriotic Building
Trinity Road
London
SW18 3SX
01-871-2016
apes 1

McGraw Hill Book Company
1221 Avenue of the Americas
New York
New York 10020
MicroExpert

Micro Data Base Systems, Inc.
P.O. Box 248
Lafayette
Indiana 47902
317-463-2581
Guru

Micro Data Base Systems, Ltd.
Imperial Building
56 Kingsway
London
WC2B 6DX
01-831-2020
Guru

PAL Software
623 Liverpool Road
Southport
PR8 3NG
061-928-6389
I1

Radian Corporation
8501 Mo-Pac Boulevard
P.O. Box 9948
Austin
Texas 78766
512-454-4797
RuleMaster

Southdata Limited
166 Portobello Road
London
W11 2EB
01-727-7564
ACLS

Software Architecture and Engineering, Inc.
1500 Wilson Boulevard
Suite 800
Arlington
Virginia 22209
703-276-7910
KES, KES 2.3

Software Architecture and Engineering
Sussex Suite
City Gates
2–4 South Gates
Chichester
West Sussex
PO19 2DJ
0243-789310
KES, KES 2.3

Systems Designers Scientific
Software Technology Centre
Pembroke House
Pembroke Broadway
Camberley
Surrey
GU15 3XD
0276-683511
Sage, Envisage

Systems Designers Software Inc.
Suite 407
444 Washington Street
Woburn
Massachusetts 01801
617-935-3070
Sage, Envisage

Teknowledge
525 University Avenue
Palo Alto
California 94301
415-327-6600
M1 Version 2

Texas Instruments Inc.
Austin
Texas 75265
800-527-3500
Personal Consultant, Personal Consultant Plus

Texas Instruments Limited
International Data Systems Division
Manton Lane
Bedford
MK41 7PA
0234-270111
Personal Consultant, Personal Consultant Plus

Warm Boot Limited
40 Bowling Green Lane
London
EC1R 0NE
01-278-0333
BEAGLE

13
Further Information

The quality of software has improved considerably during the last few years. Not only have the packages improved but also the quality of the related manuals and on-screen help. Suppliers are now aware of the impact the quality of the total package has on both image and sales. Consequently, it is worth looking at the information given out by suppliers. Rather than a brief sales pitch, information packs now contain useful information about the products and their applications. This is particularly important if you consider that most people considering the purchase of an expert systems are not experts in AI. Suppliers should give guidelines about what you can do with their products.

Nonetheless, the reader may want to look at other material for a different perspective on what experts systems are and what they will and will not do. The following is a guide to alternative sources of information.

BOOKS

The following are books that cover particular areas in greater detail than is possible in this book.

Forsyth R. (Ed.) *Expert Systems: Principles and Case Studies*; Chapman and Hall; 1984 231pp.

An interesting collection of readings including insights into Micro Expert and Reveal.

Forsyth R. and Rada R. *Machine Learning: applications in expert systems and information retrieval*; Ellis Horwood Series in Artificial Intelligence; 1986 277pp.

Covers a wide spectrum of computer applications in AI, with particular attention to the way they work.

Hayes-Roth F., Waterman D.A. and Lenat D.B. (Eds.) *Building Expert Systems*; Addison–Wesley; 1983 444pp.
A comprehensive guide to expert systems.

Holsapple C.W. and Whinston A.B. *Manager's Guide to Expert Systems Using Guru*; Dow Jones–Irwin; 1986 312pp.
A detailed look at expert systems, based on a particular package.

Nagy T., Gault D. and Nagy M. *Building Your First Expert System*; Ashton–Tate; 1985 293 pp.
Gives details about building a knowledge base using the simple shell, Micro-PS, provided on a disk with the book.

Simons G.L. *Expert Systems and Micros*; NCC Publications; 1985 247pp.
A guide to expert systems on small computers, with an extensive glossary.

OTHER BOOKS

There are a wide range of books available in the areas of expert systems and artificial intelligence. It is not necessary to read them all. However, a glance through the following list may trigger your curiosity to investigate particular aspects.

Addis T.R. *Designing Knowledge-Based Systems*; Kogan Page; 1987

Aleksander I. *Designing Intelligent Systems: An Introduction*; Kogan Page; 1984

Alty J.L and Coombs M.J. *Expert Systems: Concepts and Examples*; NCC Publications; 1984

Barr A., Cohen P. and Feigenbaum E.A. *The Handbook of Artificial Intelligence*; three volumes; Pitman; 1981,1982

Begg V. *Developing Expert CAD Systems*; Kogan Page; 1985

Bernold T. (Ed.) *Expert Systems and Knowledge Engineering*; Elsevier Science Publishers; 1986

Boose J.H. *Expertise Transfer for Expert Systems Design*; Elsevier Science Publishers; 1986

Buchanan B.G. and Shortliffe E.H. *Rule-Based Expert Systems: The MYCIN Experiments of the Stanford Heuristic Programming Project*; Addison–Wesley; 1984

Bramer M.A. (Ed.) *Research and Development in Expert Systems*: Cambridge University Press; 1985

Clancey W. *Knowledge-Based Tutoring: The GUIDON Approach*; The MIT Press; 1987

Cohn A.G. and Thomas J.R. *Artificial Intelligence and its Applications*; John Wiley and Sons; 1986

Coombs M.J. *Developments in Expert Systems*; Academic Press; 1985

CRI Directory of Expert Systems; Learned Information Ltd; 1986

Frost R.A. *Introduction to Knowledge Base Systems*; Collins; 1986

Gill K.S. *Artificial Intelligence for Society*; John Wiley and Sons; 1986

Goodall A. *The Guide to Expert Systems*; Learned Information Ltd; 1985

Harmon P. and King D. *Expert Systems: Artificial Intelligence in Business*; John Wiley and Sons; 1985

Hart A. *Knowledge Acquisition for Expert Systems*; Kogan Page; 1986

Haugeland J. *Artificial Intelligence: The Very Idea*; The MIT Press; 1985

Hewett J. and Johnson T. *Commercial Expert Systems in Europe*; Ovum Ltd; 1986

Hewett J. and Sasson R. *Expert Systems 1986*: Volume 1, USA and Canada; Ovum Ltd; 1986

Hunt V.D. *Artificial Intelligence and Expert Systems Sourcebook*; Chapman and Hall; 1986

Insight Directory of Fifth Generation Research and Development, Learned Information Ltd; 1986

Jackson P. *Introduction to Expert Systems*; Addison–Wesley; 1986

Keravnou E.T. and Johnson L. *Competent Expert Systems: A Case Study in Fault Diagnosis*; Kogan Page; 1986

Klahr P. and Waterman D.A. *Expert Systems: Techniques, Tools and Applications*; Addison–Wesley; 1986

Kidd A. (Ed.) *Knowledge Acquisition for Expert Systems: A Practical Handbook*; Plenum; 1987

Martin N. *Software Engineering of Expert Systems*; Addison–Wesley; 1987

Michie D. *On Machine Intelligence*; Ellis Horwood; 1986

Miller P.L. *A Critiquing Approach to Expert Computer Advice*; Pitman; 1984

Negoita C.V. *Expert Systems and Fuzzy Systems*; Benjamin/Cummings; 1985

Ross Quinlan J. *Applications of Expert Systems*; Addison–Wesley; 1987

Sell P.S. *Expert Systems—A Practical Introduction*; Macmillan; 1985

Shapiro A. *Structured Induction in Expert Systems*; Addison–Wesley; 1987

Simons G.L. *Is Man a Robot?*; John Wiley and Sons; 1986

Waterman D.A. *A Guide to Expert Systems*; Addison–Wesley; 1986

Weiss S.M. and Kulikowski C.A. *A Practical Guide to Designing Expert Systems*; Chapman and Hall; 1984

Wilks Y. *Artificial Intelligence Abstracts*; Basil Blackwell; 1987

Winston P.H. and Brown R.H. *Artificial Intelligence: An MIT Perspective, Two Volumes*; The MIT Press; 1982

Winston P.H. and Prendergast K.A. *The AI Business: Commercial Uses of Artificial Intelligence*; The MIT Press; 1986

SPECIALIST JOURNALS

These are journals that relate specifically to artificial intelligence and expert systems.

Artificial Intelligence; North Holland Publishing Company; The Netherlands

Artificial Intelligence Review; Blackwell Scientific Publications; UK

Expert Systems: The International Journal of Knowledge Engineering; Learned Information Ltd; UK

Expert Systems in Business; Learned Information Ltd; UK

Expert Systems User; Compass Press Publications; UK

International Journal of Expert Systems; JAI Press; UK

The Knowledge Engineering Review; British Computer Society; UK

PRODUCT UPDATES

In addition to specialist journals, most general computer journals and magazines carry articles relating to AI and expert systems. For readers who are not computer experts, the general literature may be more digestible. A few of the publications of interest are:

Byte
Personal Computer World
Practical Computing

and journals and magazines relating to your hardware such as *PC* and *PC Week*

PROFESSIONAL JOURNALS

As the new technology becomes more widespread so the professional bodies take more and more notice. This is reflected in the increasing amount of attention given to the new technology in professional journals. There are advantages in reading articles and reviews published in the journal relating to your profession. They will be written in a language you will understand and they will be about applications that are relevant to you.

CONFERENCES

Just as the number of computer journals and magazines seems to grow faster than the expert systems they write about, so the number of conferences is growing. They are generally announced in the professional and computer press.

VIDEOS

Many of us now receive a lot of our up-to-date information via television. This is reflected in the development of videos for teaching purposes. AI and expert systems have related videos available.

'AI MASTERS'

This is a series of three videos with related teaching material and manuals, which includes:

Expert Systems: Automating Knowledge Acquisition
    Donald Michie and Ivan Bratko

Machine Vision: The Advent of Intelligent Robots
Michael Brady

Logic Programming: Prolog and its Applications
Bob Kowalski and Frank Kriwaczek

The series is produced by:

Addison–Wesley Publishers Ltd. Finchampstead Road
Wokingham
Berks
RG11 2NZ
Telephone Number: 0734-794000.

'EXPERT SYSTEMS IN INDUSTRY'

This is a video produced by the Alvey Directorate in conjunction with the BBC OU Production Centre. It gives several examples of expert systems in use as well as a general introduction to the area. It is available from:

The Open University Learning Materials Service Office
The Centre for Continuing Studies
P.O. Box 188
The Open University
Milton Keynes
MK7 6DH
Telephone Number: 0908-653338

BODIES

The following are independent bodies that can give help and advice to aspiring expert system developers and users.

The Alvey Directorate
Millbank Tower
Millbank
London
SW1P 4QU

Contact: Director of Knowledge Based Systems
Telephone Number: 01-211-6108

In addition to sponsoring projects, setting up workshops and producing reports and videos on expert systems, the directorate also facilitates the setting up of Alvey Expert Systems Awareness Clubs for groups of industries or businesses, for example, TRACE is a club for transport organisations.

The British Computer Society Specialist Group on Expert Systems
13 Mansfield Street
London W1
01-637-0471

The British Computer Society has a Specialist Interest Group on Expert Systems. Membership of the group is open to anybody with an interest in this area. Membership of the Group is not confined to members of the BCS. The group provides a number of services to its members, including the organising of the UK National Conference on Expert Systems, held in Brighton in December, occasional specialist workshops, and a regular series of evening lectures. In addition, the Group publishes a quarterly newsletter and *The Knowledge Engineering Review.*

NCC
Oxford Road
Manchester
M1 7ED
061-228-6333

The National Computer Centre is a non-profit-distributing organisation backed by government and industry which provides public and in-house training materials. It produces a wide range of publications including the Expert System Starter Pack.

The Society for the Study of Artificial Intelligence and Simulation of Behaviour
Contact: Ms. Judith Dennison
Membership Secretary, SSAISB
Cognotive Studies Programme
University of Sussex
Falmer
Brighton
BN1 9QN

Now over twenty years old, the Society publishes a quarterly newsletter, jointly sponsors a biennial conference, holds a biennial summer school and organises workshops on particular issues of relevance to Artificial Intelligence research and development.

Glossary

The following are terms in common use relating specifically to expert systems. General terms relating to computer hardware and software can be found in introductory books on computing.

Algorithm
A series of structured, predefined steps for solving a particular problem. Often used as the basis for writing an imperative language computer program.

Application
What a computer does for its user and is the purpose for which it was purchased. Cf. Shell.

Artificial Intelligence
The area of computing concerned with replicating the physical and mental attributes and skills of humans.

Assertional Languages
A means of entering information into a computer so that it can be used as the basis for future applications. Cf. Imperative Languages.

Backward Chaining
Systems that work backwards through the knowledge base to determine the reasons for particular outcomes. Cf. Forward Chaining.

Backward Reasoning
The same as Backward Chaining.

Bayes' Theorem
A mathematical way of handling uncertainties in the knowledge base.

Benchmark
A means of measuring the performance of a computer or a system.

Blackboarding
A technique for combining the knowledge of several experts or several knowledge bases.

Breadth-First Search
In a hierarchically structured knowledge base, a strategy for looking at all the rules on the same level before going on to the next level. Cf. Depth-First Search.

C
An imperative language, very popular for writing expert system shells because of its speed of operation.

Chip
A piece of material, probably silicon, containing integrated circuits made up of transistor equivalents, diodes, triodes, etc.

Compatibility
The ability of one computer to run a package written for another.

Context-Sensitive Help
On-screen help given by a package, shell or application that is related to the activity currently being undertaken by the user.

Database
A collection of stored information about a domain that can be easily accessed and updated.

Dedicated System
A system bought and used for one purpose such as word processing or AI.

Deep Knowledge
Knowledge about knowledge, that is, knowing how knowledge is structured and when it can be applied. Cf. Surface Knowledge.

Disks
Magnetically-coated media capable of storing large amounts of data that can be written to and read by a computer.

Domain
An area of knowledge that can be encapsulated within an expert system knowledge base.

Dongle
An electronic key that restricts access to a computer or an application on that computer.

End User
A person who will use the expert system after it has been created and tested.

Expert
A person whose expertise in a particular domain is going to form the basis of an expert system.

Expert System
A system that uses a knowledge base to help or advise users. Either the knowledge base is rule-based or rule-inducing.

Explanation
The facility of an expert system to justify a particular course of reasoning or action to the user.

Factors
The items in a database that contribute to the rules in a rule-inducing system.

Fifth Generation
The next generation of computers, being developed largely by the Japanese, designed to use assertional languages.

FORTRAN
An imperative language, originally for mathematical applications (FORmula TRANslation), used to write expert system shells.

Forward Chaining
Systems that work forwards through the knowledge base to determine the outcome of particular sets of events or circumstances. Cf. Forward Chaining.

Forward Reasoning
The same as Forward Chaining.

Frames
A method of storing information in manageable chunks that can be accessed and used by an expert system.

Front End
Facility added to a software package or application to make it easier to use.

Fuzzy Logic
The ability to handle incomplete or uncertain information, which attempts to replicate in expert systems the way the human brain is believed to work.

Graphics Interface
The facility to link with a package to display graphically on the computer screen what is currently happening.

Heuristic
A rule-of-thumb that helps humans handle complex situations, for example, 'if it might rain, I will take an umbrella'.

Imperative Languages
Traditional computer programming languages that are used to create a set of commands to be followed by the computer. Cf. Assertional Languages.

Inference Engine
The part of an expert system that uses the knowledge base to create new facts using forward or backward chaining. Cf. Knowledge Base.

Interactive
The facility for the user to communicate directly with the system.

Interface
The link between one part of a system and another, normally between the computer and the outside world, such as the man–machine interface.

Knowledge Base
The part of an expert system that contains the rules relating to the domain of the expert system. Cf. Inference Engine.

Knowledge Base Administrator KBA
The person responsible for ensuring that a knowledge base is updated and maintained.

Knowledge Base Engineer KBE
A person with skills and experience responsible for the creation and development of a knowledge base.

LISP
An assertional programming language, written specifically to handle lists, popular in North America for AI applications.

Logic
The science of argument or proof.

Mainframe
A large computer, normally located centrally in an organisation, capable of handling very large applications.

Man–Machine Interface MMI
The manner in which the computer relates to the user, including such things as menus, windows and graphics.

Menu
A choice of on-screen options from which to choose, that reduces the need to use a keyboard and also reduces errors.

Meta Rules
Rules about rules, rules which state which group of rules can be applied. Cf. Deep Knowledge.

Natural Language
The branch of AI involved in creating systems that will allow computers to input and output in English.

Package
A program or suite of programs written for a particular purpose such as a text processing package or an expert system shell.

Partitioning
The division of a knowledge base into related sections so that future developments and maintenance are easier to carry out.

Pascal
A popular imperative language used for writing expert system shells that will run on a personal computer.

Personal Computer
A small computer dedicated to one person's use and probably sitting on their desk.

Predicate Calculus
Logic based on arguments and relations to prove given conditions are true if the given premises are true. The logical basis of rules.

Probability
The likelihood that something will happen, either measured mathematically, for example, probability = 0.5, or linguistically, for example, it is highly likely/likely/unlikely etc.

Program
A list of statements written in a particular computer language instructing the computer to perform particular tasks.

PROLOG
An assertional language, (PROgramming LOGic) used to create AI applications and expert shells, which is popular in Europe.

Real Time
A system that runs at the same time as the real world and is affected by and triggers events, such as a burglar alarm system.

Rule
A structured way of storing heuristics in a knowledge base, normally in the form: if... then...

Rule Dictionary
A guide to the rules in a knowledge base to facilitate finding and changing the rules.

Rule-Based
An expert system using a knowledge base of predefined rules to give advice or help. Cf. Rule-Inducing.

Rule-Inducing
An expert system that works out the rules from a set of examples, normally held as factors in a database. These rules can then be used to give help or advice. Cf. Rule-Based.

Rule Set
A collection of rules representing knowledge. In rule-based expert systems, the same as a Knowledge Base.

Shell
A package used by a knowledge base engineer to develop expert system applications. Cf. Application.

Surface Knowledge
Knowledge about a subject, with no implicit structure. Cf. Deep Knowledge.

Systems Life Cycle
The development process of traditional computer applications.

User
A person, generally held as non-expert, who will use an expert system application.

User Interface
The link between the user and the system, which is expected to be as friendly or helpful as possible.

Very Large Scale Integration VLSI
The facility for putting thousands of elements onto a chip to make it yet more powerful.

Why Facility
The ability of expert systems to give an explanation of their actions.

Windows

The method of dividing a computer screen into parts, each containing related but different information.

Workstation

A comprehensive, stand alone system that helps a user do their job. An AI workstation would normally run LISP or PROLOG programs.

Index